TEACHER EDUCATION PROGRAMMES THROUGH DISTANCE EDUCATION

TEACHER EDUCATION PROGRAMMES THROUGH DISTANCE EDUCATION

DHANESWAR HARICHANDAN
Professor of Education & Director,
Institute of Distance and Open Learning,
University of Mumbai,
Vidyanagiri, Mumbai-400098

DEEP & DEEP PUBLICATIONS PVT. LTD.
F-159, Rajouri Garden, New Delhi - 110027

TEACHER EDUCATION PROGRAMMES
THROUGH DISTANCE EDUCATION

ISBN 978-81-8450-259-6

Typeset by THE LASER PRINTERS, 8/15, 3rd Floor, Subhash Nagar, New Delhi-110027.

Printed in India at MAYUR ENTERPRISES
WZ Plot No. 3, Gujjar Market, Tihar Village, New Delhi - 110 018

Published by DEEP & DEEP PUBLICATIONS PVT. LTD.,
F-159, Rajouri Garden, New Delhi-110027. Phones: 25435369, 25440916.
E-mail: ddpbooks@yahoo.co.in • ddpubs@gmail.com
Sales Showroom: 2/13, Ansari Road, Daryaganj, New Delhi-110002
Phone/Fax: 23245122

Contents

Preface

As a part of the sanctioned study a nationwide survey was conducted to look into the teacher education programmes offered through distance education mode in Indian universities. There are more than 300 universities out of which 106 universities are having Distance Education Institutes (DEIs) including 10 Open Universities (OUs) in the country at present. While a large number of institutes/universities were offering teacher education programmes through correspondence/distance mode prior to the establishment of NCTE as a statutory body by the Government of India, at present there are only 11 institutes/universities (roughly 10% of the total DEIs/OUs) offering teacher education programmes through distance education mode. There is an uneven distribution of these institutes/universities offering teacher education programmes through distance education mode. While there were five institutes in the north and equal number of institutes in the south, YCMOU represents the only university in the western corridor to offer teacher education programme through distance education mode. Surprisingly not a single institute/university either in the east or in the north-east offers these programmes through distance education mode, although there are a quite number of DEIs and OUs in this part of the country.

Except IGNOU, all other DEIs and OUs restrict the admission of students to the limit of their territorial jurisdiction. Therefore, there is an urgent need to start teacher education programme through distance education mode in the northeast as well as eastern part of the country. May be some of the DEIs/OUs could be persuaded to launch teacher education programme in these parts of India.

One of the broad aims of this research study was to find out how effectively teacher education programmes could be delivered through distance education mode. Delivery of teacher education programme in this context means how curriculum transaction could take place. Since this is a professional course, the study aims to find the extent of usefulness of using distance education mode. The curriculum of teacher education programme involves practice teaching in the schools, conduct of psychological experiments and of course the pedagogy part. Some of the major findings of the study will highlight these points.

The oldest of all the institutes is Punjabi University, Patiala in Punjab, which was established in 1968. The latest one on the scenario is Shri Padmavati Mahila Vishvavidyalayam, Tirupathi in Andhra Pradesh, which was established in 1999 and is a deemed university. It is important to note that these programmes are offered only for in-service teachers.

Institutes like Andhra University, Vishakhapatnam, H.P. University, Shimla; KSOU, Karnataka; Punjabi University, Patiala and YCMOU, Nasik offer both B.Ed. and M.Ed. programmes whereas the rest of the institutions offer only B.Ed. programme. The enrolment in B.Ed. course varies from 250 to 2000 and in the M.Ed. course from 100 to 475. The higher enrolment figures is in respect of OUS only, whose jurisdiction covers the entire country in case of IGNOU, and the entire state in case of State Open Universities like Karnataka and Rajasthan.

The medium of instruction is English and the local vernacular medium like Telugu, Kannada and Marathi in A.P., Karnataka and Maharashtra respectively. In the northern belt it is English and Hindi with the exception of Punjabi University, which offers instruction in Punjabi. The enrolment is on the basis of written tests and interviews for B.Ed. and merit alone for M.Ed. In some cases weightage is given to those teachers who are having longer teaching experience in school systems.

The faculty strength varies from a minimum of 4 in Kakatiya University, to a maximum of 23 in Himachal Pradesh University. It is a good trend that all the institutions running programme through distance education mode are at least having some core faculty members to oversee the programme delivery of the course.

Most of the faculty members have a doctorate degree to their credit and are generally highly experienced.

The course materials are prepared in the self-instructional material (SIM) form in case of OUs and printed booklets and topic-wise notes in DEIs. Films, Audio-Visual Aids, Audio Cassettes and Computer Assisted Lessons supplement them. The size of SIM is usually around 200 pages, written in simple language with adequate topic coverage and bibliography.

Such is the quality of study materials of IGNOU and YCMOU that they have bagged international awards and recognition from the organisation such as COL, Canada for its standard of material production. The fact that both the teachers and students of conventional universities use the study materials of distance education programme to supplement their classroom teaching and learning speaks for their quality.

The course materials are prepared in general by a course team and evaluated by experts in the field of teacher education and distance education in relation to the relevance of content, style of presentation and language difficulty. Generally they are good hardbound booklets and their cost is included in the course fees.

As far as practice teaching goes, all the institutions insist on giving 40 lessons during the course (20 in each method). Lesson guidance is given both individually and in groups. The lessons are evaluated by teacher educators, school teachers, Principals of schools and core staff of DEIs. The students are given feedback both individually as well as in groups.

The Personal Contact Programme Lectures (PCP) are held in varying times depending on the institutions either at the beginning or at the end or in the middle of the course. The duration of PCP is usually a given time slot, which ranges from 6 days to a maximum of 15 days. The attendance is compulsory. These programmes are conducted at the contact centers, study centers or DEIs. The faculty members involved are the staff of the DEIs, visiting faculty or both.

It is also seen that the support services provided includes library with reference and lending facilities, study rooms, photocopying facilities, audio-visual aids. In YCMOU, on line guidance is also provided. The counseling is given as per the student's demand regarding the choice of papers, practice teaching, use of library, examination, confidence building, etc.

Evaluation is an ongoing process with 25 to 30 per cent weightage being given to internal assessment. It is usually done through assignments, oral and written tests, seminars and external examination. The remaining 70-75 per cent weightage is being given to term-end examination and final examination. Evaluation is continuous in both DEIs and OUs.

Assignments are compulsory for all students. The main purpose is to enhance the student learning and assessment of their performance mid-way. The students are required to submit assignments of 6-10 pages in each unit. Staff of DEIs or part time tutors evaluate the assignments. The comments given are usually individualistic in nature. The time given for submission ranges from 15 days to 6 months. The marks of these assignments are added to the final examination marks.

Thus the present research study shows that distance education, in its various forms can work and if well designed can be educationally effective. It has been applied to the education of teachers and has been shown to be effective on a number of measures. Earlier studies have indicated that the distance education programmes have often shown advantages over conventional programmes.

Even international experience shows that the governments in developing as well as developed nations of the world are using the distance education mode extensively to impart teacher education programmes. In countries such as Hong Kong, Zimbabwe and Kenya, the imparting teacher education through distance education mode has been made a part of the policy decision in education.

In our context, Distance Education has been used to teach, support and develop teachers for many years. Since the NCERT started the summer training programme for the in-service teachers during the 1960s, similar programmes could be adapted for imparting teacher education programmes through distance education mode more effectively now with the availability of new information and communication technology.

DHANESWAR HARICHANDAN

Acknowledgements

This Major Research Project was conceived in the year 1999 when NCTE abruptly discontinued the M.Ed. programme through distance education mode in Indian Universities and came out with a set of norms. When a proposal was submitted to DEC for financial grant, Prof. V.S. Prasad, the then Director of DEC encouraged me to undertake this project. I must in the first place, mention his name while expressing my acknowledgements.

My thanks are due to all the Open Universities and Distance Education Institutes who have cooperated in filling up the questionnaire sparing their time for a discussion and providing a copy of the prospectus and the study materials for the research work without whose support this report would not have been complete.

I also owe a debt of thanks to Prof. H.P. Dixit, the Chairman of DEC and the Vice Chancellor of IGNOU for allowing me extension of time to submit the project report.

My sincere thanks to Ms. Rajalakshmi K. Iyer, Research Associate of this project.

I am also thankful to my colleagues at the IDE University of Mumbai and the Director for providing infrastructure facilities for the conduct of this research.

Finally, my thanks go to my wife Swarnalata and my son Anant for their support during the long hours the research report took to complete.

DHANESWAR HARICHANDAN

Acronyms

ADB	Asian Development Bank
B.Ed.	Bachelor of Education
BJET	British Journal of Educational Technology
CIDA	Canadian International Development Agency
CIE	Central Institute of Education
COL	Commonwealth of Learning
DEC	Distance Education Council
DEI	Distance Education Institute
DFID	Department for International Development
DIET	District Institute of Education and Training
ICT	Information and Communication Technology
IGNOU	Indira Gandhi National Open University
KSOU	Karnataka State Open University
M.Ed.	Master of Education
NCERT	National Council of Educational Research and Training
NCTE	National Council for Teacher Education
OU	Open University
PCP	Personal Contact Programme
SBTE	Secondary Board of Teacher Education
SIM	Self-Instructional Material
UK	United Kingdom
UNESCO	United Nations Educational Scientific and Cultural Organisation
USA	United States of America
USSR	Union of Soviet Socialist Republics
YCMOU	Yashwantrao Chavan Maharashtra Open University

CHAPTER

1

Introduction

1.0 THE BACKGROUND

The origin and development of teacher education in India dates back to the early nineteenth century. English education was introduced in formal schools, which made it necessary for teachers to teach something that was quite new to them. A quick look at the way teacher education has evolved indicates that there have been three significant developments. *First,* there was a physical growth in terms of number of institutions; this process has been fairly continuous from the pre-independence period although tremendous expansion has taken place during the post-independence period too. *Second,* diversification of teacher education programmes took place across different stages of education such as pre-school, primary, secondary and higher secondary. This occurred during the pre-independence period for the primary and secondary stages, while its spread to higher secondary and pre-primary are essentially recent developments. *Third,* teacher education emerged in specific areas of specialization like science education, mathematics education, special education, art education, physical education, language teaching, etc. As a result of these developments, teacher education today has become a significant component of our educational system with a large-scale network of various institutions and an area of academic specialisation.

With this background we will see briefly how teacher education programme has unfolded during pre-independence period and post-independence period. It will not be out of context if we further glance at the teacher education programme in some other countries of the world having similar kind of situations as that of India and the role of some international agencies working in the field of education especially in teacher education sector.

1.1 TEACHER EDUCATION IN PRE-INDEPENDENCE PERIOD

It is pertinent to have an overview of how these developments in teacher educations have evolved. The initial attempts formally made towards teacher education programme seems to have been by some private agencies in the three Presidencies under the East India Company during the early decades of the eighteenth century. State initiative ensured towards the end of the eighteenth century and an aftermath of the government assuming responsibility for education in India. Government initiative in teacher education came only as a consequence of Wood's Despatch of 1854. Wood's Despatch recognized the great deficiency in the facilities for teachers' training and desired to see the establishment with as little delay as possible of training.

The establishment of universities after 1857 led to an increase in the number of colleges. This development had an impact on normal schools. In view of the expansion and diversification that had taken place in the educational system, the Indian Education Commission (1882) provided some definite directions for furthering teacher education in India. The Commission not only approved of teacher training programmes for both elementary and secondary school teachers, but also recommended a separate programme for secondary school, distinctly higher in level, form and method.

The commission also recommended separate training programmes for graduates and undergraduates. As a sequel to this report, training colleges were established for the first time and soon six training colleges came into existence. Thus, by the end of the nineteenth century, teacher education became established as a substantial structural set-up. The onset of the twentieth century ushered in a period of real transition in the field of education. The Saddler Commission Report (1917-19) laid stress on substantially increasing the output of trained teachers. *It recommended that a Department of Education should be created in the Universities of Dacca and Calcutta and that education should be included as a subject of study in Intermediate, B.A. and M.A. degree examinations.*

Hartog Committee Report (1929) led to the setting up of in-service education programmes for primary school teachers. Sergent Committee in 1944 recommended that provision should be made for training different categories of teachers, refresher courses should be organized for giving in-service education to teachers, and teaching practice should be strengthened. *Meanwhile in-service training in the form of short-term courses, evening classes, summer school courses, etc. were started.*

With the emerging knowledge base of what could be called 'Education', a more theoretical study of it at the postgraduate level came to be pursued as an M.Ed. Degree.

On the whole, by the time of independence teacher education had been established as one distinct component of the educational system. It was recognized as necessary for school teachers, both elementary and the secondary. There were several institutions engaged in providing teacher training. Full time pre-service teacher training programmes were initiated. The idea of in-service teacher training for updating the technical knowledge and skills of working teacher had began to emerge. Training programmes got differentiated to suit the requirements of elementary and secondary school teachers.

1.2 TEACHER EDUCATION IN POST-INDEPENDENCE PERIOD

Major strides have been made in teacher education since Independence. Form being a mere training component, it has become an essential aspect of the educational system. Looking back on the development over the years, three streams of action seem to have been undertaken:

(i) expansion of pre-service teacher education;
(ii) opening of supplementary channels for clearing the backlog of untrained teachers; and
(iii) expansion of in-service teacher education.

The expansion of pre-service teacher education is impressive if one looks at the continuous growth in the number of teacher education institutes. From a mere 10 secondary teacher training institutions in 1948, the number increased to 50 in 1965 and 633 in 1995 (NCTE). There has also been a phenomenal growth of teaching profession in India since independence. During 1994-95, about 4.3 million teachers were working in different levels of schools. Of these, 2.7 million (66 per cent) were engaged in primary and upper primary schools.

The incidence of backlog of 'untrained teachers' has persisted from pre-independence times. It was due to inadequate teacher education facilities during the pre-independence period and the compulsion to employ a large number of teachers, with or without training, in order to make schools accessible across wider regions of the country. One measure adopted was the practice of deputing untrained school teachers to training colleges. While this practice maintained the continuity of effort at clearing the backlog, its actual contribution was not very substantial.

The Education Commission (1964-66) recognised in strong terms the urgent need to clear the backlog of untrained teachers and *recommended opening supplementary channels. Summer courses, part time courses and correspondence courses were suggested by the commission as effective possibilities.* Around the same time, a part time B.Ed. Programme was introduced in some institutions enrolling only working teachers. These teachers worked full time in schools and during evenings attended classes. The duration of the programme was extended to two years with the content being the same as that of the regular full time course.

One more programme was introduced, which is commonly known as *'Vacation Courses'*. Under this programme, working teachers went through teacher education programme for sixteen weeks during two summer vacations of eight weeks each. During this period, nearly 100-120 days of theoretical study would be completed and the practice component would be completed in one's own school. Different institutions conduct this programme differently with regard to the supervision of practice lessons and feedback. They include teacher educators visiting schools according to the time and date convenient to them as well as the student teacher, selective supervision by teacher educators, supervision by the school principal and teacher educators, and supervision by the school principal only.

During sixties another channel, i.e. ***correspondence courses*** was introduced. The correspondence-*cum*-contact mode was considered suitable especially for teachers of the secondary school stage. In order to institutionalise this mode of teacher training, the Central Institute of Education, then a constituent of NCERT, started in 1966 a B.Ed. programme through the correspondence-*cum*-contact mode.

Though these five institutions, i.e. the Central Institute of Education and the four Regional Colleges of Education, now Regional Institute of Education have since given up the programme, their involvement along with their academic credibility were instrumental in making programmes of secondary school teacher education through the correspondence mode more widespread. Another factor that gave impetus to correspondence courses was the three delegations of experts sent by the University Grants Commission to the erstwhile USSR during 1967-69, to study the system of correspondence courses and suggest the suitability of this channel for India. This delegation made positive recommendations and included 'teacher training' as one of the areas in which courses through correspondence mode could be offered to begin with. During the seventies and later, such courses leading to a B.Ed. degree, have been instituted by many universities. By 1996, the number had increased to twenty-four.

The way correspondence courses have expanded and have been implemented leaves much to be desired. They have assumed the status of an 'alternative' channel, deviating from the original supplementary role of reaching out to those who cannot be accommodated in regular training institutions. On one hand, they have drawn in large numbers, and on the other, they have come in for a lot of criticism for vitiating the quality of teacher education and making it commercialized.

However, another trend that seems to have emerged during the last two decades is in terms of modes of curriculum transaction. If clearance of backlog untrained teachers and provision of teacher education programme for certain special groups represent fields/specific needs, the institutions of correspondence courses, and now their *improved forms such as distance education programmes represent steps for making teacher education more responsive to field needs.* Recent trends towards developing open and distance learning systems represent efforts to explore more varied and effective modes for curriculum transaction as well as imparting teacher education programmes effectively.

An expert committee appointed by the NCTE under the chairmanship of Prof. R.C. Das (1995) felt that:

> "If part time face-to-face institutional programmes are equivalent to face-to-face full time institutional programmes in their total duration of instruction, programmes and academic staff support and other infrastructure as per National Council for Teacher Education norms, then the National Council for Teacher Education may consider their recognition after obtaining detailed information from these institutions."

As per the present sanction, the NCTE recognises correspondence/distance mode as a viable mode of imparting teacher education programmes.

1.3 TEACHER EDUCATION PROGRAMME ABROAD

The world needs better teachers and more teachers. The Dakar conference revealed that there were still more than 100 million children out of school. They need teachers as the world moves towards the 2015 target of education for all. And we need to raise the skills of the existing 600 million teachers, too many of whom are untrained and unqualified. Beyond that, the skills and knowledge of all teachers needs are no longer fixed and familiar but moving ones. Teachers therefore need more opportunities than ever before to go on learning throughout their careers. *One of the ways of strengthening the teaching profession is to use distance education or open and distance learning.*

Distance Education throughout the world has expanded enormously during the two past decades and teachers account for a significant number of learners. The history behind the use of teacher education by distance differs between the north and the south. In industrialized countries, where distance education is just one option within a highly developed educational system, its use in teacher education has been fairly limited and mainly to reach remote learners. But the growing legitimisation of distance education, market forces in higher education and use of new educational technologies have led to an expansion in this field. New information and communication technology in particular have opened up a range of new opportunities for course and resourse-based learning in teacher education.

There is increasing and strong interest among *governments, institutions, international agencies and teachers themselves in the use of open and distance education methods and technologies for initial training and continuing professional development of teachers.* The last decade has seen considerable growth in the number and diversity of distance education programmes, the integration of distance education with traditional and new initiatives using ICT. These trends are prompted by the need to meet teacher shortages, the demand for more continuing education for teachers in a changing world, the shift of attention from quantity to quality by policy-makers and planners, the introduction of new teacher education standards as countries progress, a search for improved training approaches and the imperative of finding new ways of using scarce resources.

Teachers throughout the world are experiencing an unprecedented transition in their role and status and demands on them are becoming increasingly multifaceted. Many teachers do not have the training on experience to cope with this changing role.

At least 1% of the world's population works as teachers in the formal education system alone with (in OECD country about 3% of the labour force is teachers) two-thirds of the world's teachers live in developing countries. Between 1970 and 1988, the total number of teachers employed in formal education increased from 25.5 to 44.1 million and by the mid-1990s it reached 60 million. For governments and societies, this represents a huge task of human resource development.

International agencies, such as the World Bank, UNESCO, the ADB, the COL, and donor's such as the DFID, UK, the Canadian

International Development Agency (CIDA) and Ausaid are giving new emphasis to distance education in their policies and plans for teacher education. Distance education is appearing more often as an option in the strategic planning of government and traditional teacher training colleges.

As a result, policy-makers and planners at several levels (international, national, provincial, and institutional) are in need of up to date information about the use of open and distance learning for teacher education and some guidance in its application. Such information can be difficult to find because reports of experience are scattered over many sources like, project reports, institutional documents published/unpublished or restricted to the level of description. We have therefore provided in the appendix the following teacher training programmes through distance education mode as was available from the internet.

1. The Organisation of Teacher Training at a Distance: The case of Kenya—Appendix I.
2. Pre-service Teacher Education at a Distance: The case of Zimbabwe—Appendix II.
3. Distance Education for Teacher Education: Hong Kong Experience—Appendix III.
4. Distance Education in the E-9 Countries: India—Appendix IV.
5. Revised Schemes of Teacher Education in India—Appendix V.
6. Media and Technology Uses in Teacher Education—Appendix VI.
7. Teacher Education Institutions recognised by NCTE—Appendix VII.

1.4 RESEARCH QUESTIONS

As the present study attempts to describe the system as it is an obvious starting point for focusing is to try and set out research questions which should suggest not only the field of study but also the methods for carrying out the research and the kind of analysis required.

The following are some of the research questions that obviously come to the researcher's mind.

- What constitutes the course materials supplied to students of teacher education programmes through distance education mode?
- What media are combined to constitute course materials?
- What is the size and volume of the supplied printed materials?
- What is the duration of personal contact programmes and practice teaching lessons?
- What is the coverage of topics during PCP Lectures?
- Whether assignments are made compulsory?
- How are the response sheets evaluated?
- How are the practice teaching lessons delivered and supervised?

These are some of the questions the answer of which have been tried out in this research reports.

1.5 NEED AND SIGNIFICANCE OF THE STUDY

Research in distance education is less focused on the teacher and more on the materials and means of transmission. Review of related literature shows few studies on Teacher Education through distance education mode and almost nil at the national level. Hence the researcher felt the need to study in detail the profile of the NCTE recognised open universities and distance education institutes in India offering teacher education programme through distance education mode.

The findings of the study would throw light on the functioning of the OU's and DEI's, try to find lacunae if any in the programme delivery and offer suitable suggestions to improve the system.

1.6 STATEMENT OF THE PROBLEM

The problem under investigation is entitled as "A study of

teacher education programmes offered through distance education mode in Indian universities."

1.7 BROAD AIMS OF THE STUDY

As the present study attempts to describe and analyse the details of *programme delivery of Teacher Education Programme* at the all India level the study will primarily look into the existing system of development of study material, organisation of personal contact programme, conduct of practice teaching and the procedure of assignment submission and assessment.

1.8 OBJECTIVES OF THE STUDY

The specific objectives of the study are as follows:

1. To examine the printed study materials: volumes, coverages and the media mix packages used, etc.
2. To study the organization of personal contact programmes for the conduct of lectures and practice teaching lessons.
3. To find out the process of submission and assessment of response sheets.
4. To suggest measures for improving the programme delivery of Teacher Education Programme.

1.9 OPERATIONAL DEFINITIONS

Teacher Education Programme

Teacher Education means programmes of educational research or training of persons for equipping them to teach at pre-primary, primary, secondary and senior secondary, stages in schools and Colleges.

In the present study Teacher Education Programme refer to the teacher training programme at the level of B.Ed. and M.Ed. only.

Distance Education

Distance Education means education offered from a distance in which there is very little face to face interaction between the teacher and the taught. It is a process of teaching and learning, where the learner is 'quasi-permanently' separated from the teacher and peer group, and teaching is done usually through self-instructional materials (both print and non-print) and communication technology with an emphasis on supported self-study.

Universities

Universities are institutions of higher learning with postgraduate teaching and research facilities constituting post-graduate department and professional colleges that award master's degrees and doctorates and an undergraduate division that awards bachelor's degrees.

In the present content, the universities/institutes which are recognised by the UGC and also by the NCTE are considered.

1.10 LIMITATIONS OF THE STUDY

The study considers the profile of the universities and programme details with respect to enrolment procedure, staff profile, conduct of personal contact programme lectures, study materials, practice teaching, etc.

The study is limited to the NCTE approved Universities and DEIs in India. Also the perception of the students about the programme and the problems they encounter are not considered. The study is limited to the Teacher Education programme of B.Ed. and M.Ed. only offered through Distance Education mode.

CHAPTER

2

Review of Related Literature

2.0 INTRODUCTION

This chapter deals with the need and importance of review of related literature followed by a brief review of the theoretical papers, articles, research reports, dissertations, etc. Obviously only those portions of the literature reviewed that have relevance to this study are presented here.

2.1 NEED AND IMPORTANCE OF REVIEW OF RELATED LITERATURE

A review of previous literature on the topic under consideration is an essential component of research. It demonstrates an understanding of the existing literature pertinent to the study under investigation. Review helps in surveying related studies and analyse them critically and put them logically to form a framework. Based on this a researcher can look for missing links in the chain of knowledge continuum and initiate work on these gaps. Some of the answers to the research questions may also be obtained from the researches that have already been conducted. It also helps in supporting and justifying the need for a study. In this chapter an attempt is made to project the literature available in the country and abroad on Teacher Education through Distance Education Mode.

2.2 STUDIES IN INDIA

In Buch's Survey of Research in Education, the following studies have been reported:

Khan, Nielofar (1991), Effectivity of distance education programme with reference to the teacher training course, Kashmir University. (Ph.D. Education, Kashmir University)

Khan, Nielofar (1991), reported that there was a year-wise increase in the enrolment from 1977-78 to 1988-89 of B.Ed. students in distance education in Kashmir University when compared to the formal system. In the Distance Education stream there was a high rise of state-wise enrolments of B.Ed. students when compared with the formal system. The pass percentage of both streams were equal.

During 1977-78 pass percentage ratio between Non-Formal and Formal system was 60:63.5.

During 1988-89 pass percentage ratio between Non-Formal and Formal system was 62:65.

The teaching competency of the teachers trained through the formal system was better than that of those trained through the distance mode. The per capita cost in the distance mode was found to be less when compared to the formal channel.

Pugazhenthi, G. (1991), "A study of teacher education programme through the correspondence system in Madurai Kamraj University" (Ph.D. Education, M.S. University, Baroda).

Upretti, D.C. (1988), Impact of teacher training through correspondence course on upward occupational mobility of the elementary teacher in the western region. Independent study in Regional College of Education, Bhopal.

These studies, in addition to other factors, also explored the characteristics and aspirations of distance learners, who had joined teacher education programmes through the distance education mode.

Upretti (1988) found that the majority of distance learners joining B.Ed. through correspondence courses had graduated in humanities and social sciences with low percentage of marks at school and college levels. A positive relationship between learner's characteristics and success in distance learning at B.Ed. level was reported by Gautam, R. (1990). In the study of Pugazhenthi (1991) the age of teacher training in the distance mode ranged from 25-65 years. Also a sizeable students both at the B.Ed. and M.Ed. level were from the rural background.

Rajendra Prasad, D. and John, E.A. (1992), *Development of skills through teaching practice—a comparative study of the attitudes of B.Ed. trainees of distance and conventional institutions, Kakatiya Journal of Distance Education, 1(2), 80-91.*

Objectives

The present study was conducted with the objectives of finding out:

- Guidance given for practice teaching by teacher educators.
- Self-preparation of the trainees for teaching practice.
- Supervision of teaching practice.
- Achievement of objectives of teaching practice.

Method

A stratified sample of 120 B.Ed. teacher trainees of Kakatiya University was selected. Equal weightage was given to distance and conventional (formal) institutions. Further, equal weightage was given to enrolled trainees of both government and private colleges from among conventional institutions. An opinionnaire, prepared by observing teaching practice of trainees and informal discussions with the supervisors of teaching practice, was administered in order to collect data.

Findings

It was found that the level of perception and performance of the B.Ed. trainees of distance education was same as that of the trainees of conventional institutions. The trainees felt that sufficient guidance had been provided to them regarding teaching practice. But majority of them preferred materials prepared in regional language. The distance trainees were found to have more control over classroom situation so as to make students more disciplined than the trainees of conventional institutions. Majority of the teaching practice classes lacked adequate seating arrangements. Trainees from both conventional and distance institutions could not use sufficient charts and 3-dimensional aids. But it was remarkable to note that the distance trainees performed better in experimental demonstration in comparison to their counterparts of conventional institutions. The results showed that the trainees of distance education were in no way inferior to their counterparts in conventional institutions with regard to level of perception, self-preparation and achievement of objectives of practice teaching.

Srinivas, Rashmi (1992), *Teacher Training through the Distance Mode: An Approach to the Teaching of Grammar, M. Litt. Dissertation, Central Institute of English and Foreign Languages, Hyderabad.*

Objectives

The major objective of the study was to examine the grammar component of the existing materials for high school teachers—a 12 month correspondence course—to identify:

- Whether they fulfilled the requirement of the grammar component of the course, i.e. whether they:
  - — improve the teacher's own communicative competence,
  - — improve his/her knowledge of the language,
  - — provide him/her suggestions/guidelines on how to teach grammar at the school level,
- What kind of approach was being adopted for the teaching of grammar, i.e. whether it is a format-based approach or a semantic approach.
- Whether they were effective as self-instructional materials which the trainees can work through effectively on their own.

Method

The objectives were broken into three stages. In the first stage the trainees and their needs were identified. The views of distance learners were obtained on the appropriateness of the content, format and presentation of the materials. Also the views of subject specialists were obtained on the appropriacy of the content and the format. The learners' needs were identified through three methods—questionnaire, interview and analysis of trainees' own written English.

In stage two, effort was made to find out whether the grammar materials fulfilled the needs of the trainees. Three sample lessons were prepared on the basis of the suggestions made by the analysis. In stage three, the three sample lessons were tested.

Findings

The study presented an argument in favour of the teaching of grammar in consonance with the current theories of language learning and advocated a semantic approach to the teaching of grammar. On the basis of the profile of the trainee, his/her real perceived needs, and the semantic approach, the adequacy of the in-service teacher training correspondence course materials was established. The inadequacy was identified in terms of its weakness not merely as distance learning materials but also as teacher training materials. It was therefore suggested that the course may be improved by carrying out certain modifications in the existing materials. To demonstrate the feasibility of these modifications, three sample lessons incorporating the suggested modifications were produced as part of the study to investigate the need for further modifications for improvement. A tryout was also conducted. The tryout yielded certain suggestions for further modifications.

Arun, Renu (1990), *A Study of Success in Distance Learning System in Relation to Some Key Learner and Institutional Variables,* Doctoral Dissertation, Kurukshetra University, Kurukshetra.

Objectives

- To identify background characteristics of distance learners, reasons behind joining the B.Ed. through correspondence course, delineating profiles of distance learners in terms of key psychological variables namely self-images, learner orientation, interpersonal relations and learning strategies.
- To evaluate the effectiveness of institutional components as existing in the institute of Correspondence Education, University of Jammu, comparing distance learners and full time B.Ed. trainees in terms of completion rate,

dropout rate, percentage and quality of results, and studying the attitude of distance learners towards distance education.

- To study the relationship between learner and institutional variables with respect to success in distance learning, and to predict success of distance learning system on the basis of learner variables.

Method

All 3314-distance learners doing B.Ed. through ICE, University of Jammu were included in the sample. The data were collected by using the five tools namely, proforma for the identification data (including reasons behind joining the correspondence course); learners' orientation inventory; evaluation scale for instructional material; attitude scale for distance learning system; and proforma for dropouts. All these tools were developed by the researcher. Along with these, some other tools like Interpersonal Relations Inventory, Learning Strategies Inventory and Personality Word List were also used for collection of data.

Findings

(i) Background Variables

Information was collected from 630 distance learners regarding background variables. Out of 630 learners, three-fourth were married and those who were above the age of 30 years constituted 60 per cent of sample. 68 per cent of the candidates were from rural background, taking greater advantage of B.Ed. course through correspondence. However, only five per cent candidates had a first division in their previous university examination and 74 per cent distance learners were first generation distance learners.

Ansari, M.M. and Dash, N.K., "Managing and Financing Teacher education using distance mode: A study", Journal of Distance Education, Volume X, No. 12003, D.D.E. University of Jummu.

In pursuance of the objectives of universalization of elementary education, there has been considerable expansion in institutional infrastructure of the school system, which has profound impact on teacher demand. As the out come of schooling is seen and felt in every walk of life, the social demand for education are reflected in rising enrolment trends has far exceeded the supply of trained teachers. The growth in knowledge and technology induced changes in the process of teaching learning, required preparation of a large number of teachers who could effectively utilized educational technology for imparting quality education. Inability to meet the demand for teachers is the major factor responsible for deterioration in quality of education, heavy dropout and low level of learning attainments. It is because of the reason that the realization of constitutions objective of providing free and compulsory education to all has remain elusive and hope for creation of the culture of the life long learning is adversely affected. The situation poses a major threat to the national endeavours to create and enlightened and prosperous society.

We all know that the world enters the knowledge area. The policy makers world wide grapple with challenges of the stimulating education-led economic growth and social progress. Most developing countries including India find their capacity to respond to such challenges undermined by lack of most basic resources—teachers. Their ability to participate in this knowledge era and to meet the target of education for all would depend on their success in training new teachers upgrading existing teachers and extending the reach of all qualified teachers. The task is urgent, but the traditional system of teacher training is not duly responsive to the need for coping with the large number of under and unqualified teachers. As the teachers training methods and the approaches are being upgraded and improved to cater for a larger number and to provide a quality education, the programme should be designed such as to extend the benefits of distance education to the training and upgrading of teachers. In view of this, this paper has twin objectives, one is to identify the major problem and issue in management and financing of teacher education and other is to discuss the role of distance education in promotion of teacher education.

2.3 STUDIES ABROAD

Creed, Charlotte (2001), "The use of distance education for teachers, report for DFID by International Research Foundation for Open Learning".

This report, commissioned by the Department for International Development, was designed to map the current use of distance education for teachers, looking for evidence internationally but drawing in particular from experience in the south. Its purpose is to see how far distance education can help with the problems of teacher shortage, gender imbalance, and teaching quality that have a bearing on meeting the international education for all targets.

The organisation, curriculum and technology of distance education can all contribute to its success. In terms of organisation the more successful programmes appear to have been those in which the purpose has been coherent and has sought to integrate distance and conventional approaches. Interactive technologies, moves towards a participatory approach and diversification to match specific audience needs have all produced positive outcomes. Integration has been sought by offering equivalence programmes, by using it to support conventional programme and by providing mixed-mode education in which students spend part of their time working conventionally and part at a distance. Any of these approaches to integration makes demands for changes in the roles, and even the culture, of the various stakeholders in teacher education. A range of different organizational and supervision of classroom practice is of central importance while the models direct attention to the location of responsibility among the partners responsible for a distance-education programme.

Curricula are shaped by national and international pressures; many appear to be in transition with a tension between conventional teacher-centred and revisionist learner-centred tendencies. Distance-education programmes vary in the emphasis they given to general education, subject skills, pedagogy and practical classroom work. Distance-education approaches may make heavy demands on trainee teachers with limited learning skills or capacity in the language of instruction. While national capacity to develop materials may be restricted, there is only limited experience of international development and sharing.

In terms of technology, print continues to dominate despite the range of experiment with, and publicity about, new information and communication technologies. Other technologies used include the use of cassettes, radio, and television, especially in high-population countries, and video-conferencing. The new technologies are being used for the distribution of materials, to a limited extent for two-way communication, and for making web-based resources available to teachers.

The cost of distance education behave differently from the cost of conventional education and are likely to have relatively high fixed and low variable allowing economics of scale. Where distance education makes it possible to reduce the cost of residence, or allow trainees to work in the classroom as they study, this reduces the comparative cost of approach. Distance education has tended to be funded by Governments, through there are examples of some of the cost being met from student fees and more rarely, from the private sector. Models have been developed for the analysis of the costs of distance and conventional education. The record provides only limited data on the cost to be expected for each of the available technologies but does establish that student support, including the supervision of classroom practices, has often demanded between a quarter and a half of the total budget. Global comparisons between distance and conventional approaches suggest that above a threshold distance approaches are likely to be at an economic advantage.

Peter E. Kinyanjui, "The Organisation of Teacher Training at a Distance with Particular Reference to Kenya", Report to World Bank.

Many countries have used distance education for teacher training. This article focuses on such programmes in Kenya.

As developing countries continue to grapple with the problem of quantitative expansion of education for all people, the qualitative improvement of education at all levels, and the contingent issue of the cost of education, they must seriously consider alternative delivery systems. In this quest, distance education should play new and expanded roles. A distance education system that may have started as a stop-gap measure and then developed as an alternative system may become an integral part of the mainstream education delivery system. It may just be a matter of time.

Chivore, B.R.S. (1992), "Pre-Service Teacher Education at a Distance: The Case of Zimbabwe", Report to World Bank.

As in many countries, Zimbabwe faced a demand for teachers that far outstripped the supply from conventional colleges. This example of a pre-service teacher education programme may be useful to educators in other countries.

Since attaining its independence, Zimbabwe has invested heavily in education. In the process of that investment, the government has introduced various types of teacher education programmes. Prominent among them was the ZINTEC Programme, which brought with it distance education as a mode of training pre-service, non-graduate teachers. This innovation affected all forms of pre-service, non-graduate teacher education, in that for the first time in the country's history distance education played a prominent role in teacher education. What is now urgently required is a systematic and thorough impact evaluation of teachers trained since independence to assess their effectiveness. This is crucial because if money spent producing incompetent, inefficient, and ineffective educators it is money wasted.

Ronnie Carr, Yvonne Fung and Shui Kin Chan (2002), "Distance Education for Teacher Education: Hong Kong experience".

The Open University of Hong Kong (OUHK) is one of an increasing number of institutions offering teacher education programmes through distance education. This article focuses largely on one of the programmes from the OUHK's School of Education and Language, the in-service Bachelor of Education (Honours) in Primary Education (BEDHPE). Some examples of teacher education programmes at a distance are discussed, followed by a brief of the nature of in-service teacher education, and the feature of high-quality distance education materials and learner support systems. The articles then present the result of an evaluation of the above programme. On the basis of survey findings, it is argued that distance education programmes that are well designed and efficiently implemented can provide an effective, flexible alternative to the traditional approach to in-service teacher education.

2.4 RATIONALE OF THE STUDY

Further research is needed if distance education is to be used to maximum effectiveness. There is a shortage of good research and a need to raise the capacity of researchers. Existing literature does not tell us enough about comparative effectiveness or the most effective development of technologies. A set of issues about good management of distance education, and about its integration with conventional approach demand attention. Many of the key research questions, about curriculum and about strategies for change, among others, form part of the broader research agenda for teacher education. One neglected need is for research on the appropriate use of distance education for secondary-school teachers, including those trained at primary level but working in junior-secondary schools.

Research in Teacher Education dose not have a long past. It is only about three decades that research in this area began to be undertaken. Although the quantum of research in teacher education is increasing progressively, it leaves much to be desired in terms of the range of teacher education variables and quality. Analysing the researches conducted so far, the gap becomes quite conspicuous.

In the case of in-service teacher education little research is available regarding the use of distance learning techniques apart from evaluation studies conducted in the NCERT for the SITE, INSAT, and Radio Utilisation Project. As these modalities are being increasingly used, researches will be fruitful for providing an empirical base for their effective utilisation.

From the above review it is obvious that most of the studies in teacher education have dealt with single institutions and are focused on either the presage variables or the process variables. None of them have looked comprehensively into the question of how to improve the quality of the course materials, PCP, evaluation of response sheets for Teacher Education Programme and consequently the quality of distance education in India. Micro and macro-level studies not pertaining to M.Ed. course have been conducted by Anand (1979), Khan (1989), Sahoo (1985), Rathore (1993), Gupta (1975), Biswal (1979), and Dutt (1985). But so far no attempt has been made to study the Teacher Education course through distance education mode at national level. Hence the present nationwide investigation has been undertaken to answer the questions raised in the context of Teacher Education through the distance mode and also to examine some of the important aspects and issues taken up by previous studies to strengthen the existing system.

CHAPTER

3

Research Design

3.0 INTRODUCTION

Research design is a blue print of the proposed study which details the salient features of the envisaged research in terms of procedure, tools and techniques. This blueprint contains the outline of the details that are vital to the completion of the project undertaken.

3.1 METHODOLOGY

The present study used survey methodology of the descriptive, qualitative type, describing and interpreting what is?

The word "survey" means to view comprehensively and in detail. In another sense it refers specifically to the act of "obtaining data for mapping". The term survey is generally used for the type of research which proposes to ascertain what is the normal or typical condition or practice at the present time. What is distinctive about the survey in its combination of a commitment to a breadth of study, a focus on the snapshot at a given point of time and a dependence on empirical data.

According to Best, "the survey involves a clearly defined problem and definite objective. It requires expert and imaginative planning, careful analysis and interpretation of the data gathered and logical and skillful reporting of the findings" (Best, 1978).

In order to achieve the objectives of the present study, survey method of descriptive, qualitative type was used as this was found to be the most appropriate method to study the programmes of teacher education offered through distance education mode in Indian universities.

In this study the researcher has:

(i) identified the various NCTE approved OUs and DEIs offering Teacher Education Programme through distance education mode,
(ii) described the profile of the various selected institutions in detail, and
(iii) analysed and interpreted the available data qualitatively.

3.2 SAMPLE

Being a census study all the NCTE approved OUs and DEIs in India, conducting teacher education programmes through distance education mode were considered. In all 11 DEIs and OUs formed sampling frame which is given in Table 3.1.

TABLE 3.1

Sampling Frame

Total No. of Institutes Offering Teacher Education Programme through Education Mode	*Total No. of Institutes Selected for the Study*	*Percentage*
11	11	100

The list which forms the population as well as the sample of the study was obtained from the website of NCTE as on 2004 and is presented in Table 3.2.

TABLE 3.2

Teacher Education Institutes in India Offering Programmes through Distance Education Mode

Name of the University	*Name of the DEI/OU*
Kakatiya University, Warangal	School of Distance Learning and Continuing Education
S.V. University, Tirupati	Shri Padmavati Mahila Distance Vishvavidyalayam
S.V. University, Tirupati	Directorate of Distance Education
Andhra University, Vishakhapatnam	School of Distance Learning and Continuing Education
Himachal Pradesh University, Shimla	International Centre for Distance Education and Open Learning
IGNOU, New Delhi	School of Education
Karnataka State Open University, Mysore	Department of Studies and Research in Education
Kota Open University, Kota	School of Education
M.D. University, Rohtak	Department of Distance Education
Punjabi University, Patiala	Department of Correspondence Courses
YCMOU, Nashik	School of Education

3.3 TOOL

The selection of suitable instruments or tools is of vital importance for successful research. Questionnaire is one such tool used extensively by researchers especially in survey method.

A questionnaire can be defined as a systematic compilation of questions that are submitted to a sampling of population from which cooperation is solicited. Questionnaire falls under data gathering devices, which make use of properly prepared forms for inquiring into and securing information under study. Questionnaire is a simple and clear device to get objective results in the best possible way.

As the present study is a census study of the qualitative, descriptive type, questionnaire was obviously the most suitable tool for gathering data. So an institutional questionnaire was prepared and duly validated by experts in the field of Education and Distance Education. After validation, some items were revised as per the suggestions of the experts, some were ignored and some new one's got included.

The final tool consisted of 11 questions in all, each question with sections and sub-sections, regarding profile of the institutions, the courses conducted, admission norms and procedures, medium of instruction, profile of the faculty, self-instructional materials, library facilities, personal contact programmes, practice teaching lessons, assignments and their evaluation, counseling services offered, etc.

3.4 DATA COLLECTION

It can be often heard in the research circles that if data collection is complete, 80% of your job is done!! How true this cliché is, the researcher and his colleagues realized the hard way! The process turned out to be an arduous one. The researcher and his colleagues visited each of the selected institutions and the questionnaire was personally administered to the concerned institutions. The data were collected during March to June 2004 by visiting the institutes personally. Some of the institutes were even visited twice on return journey since the entire data could not be obtained during the first visit.

Besides, during the visit to the institutes a set of study materials, prospectus and other related guidelines about the conduct of these teacher education programmes were also collected. Some of these on payment basis others were complimentary. But with the exception of Karnataka State Open University, YCMOU, Nashik, Vardhman Mahavir Open University, Kota and Punjabi University, Patiala from where completely filled in questionnaires were received, the other institutions were not all that cooperative. In fact two of the DEIs from Andhra Pradesh refused to oblige even after repeated reminders and phone calls. In such cases, the researcher has relied upon secondary sources such as leaflets, prospectus, website, etc.

So ultimately with the exception of IGNOU, New Delhi, Shri Padmavati Distance Vishvavidyalayam, Tirupati and Directorate of Distance Education S.V. University, Tirupati, the data (both

Primary and Secondary) collected has been tabulated, analysed and interpreted.

TABLE 3.3

Number of Institutes Visited for Administering Questionnaire

No. of Institutes visited for administering Questionnaire	*Response received*	*Response not received*
11	08 (73%)	03 (27%)

The following pie chart in Figure 3.1 shows the percentage of response received and not received.

Figure 3.1

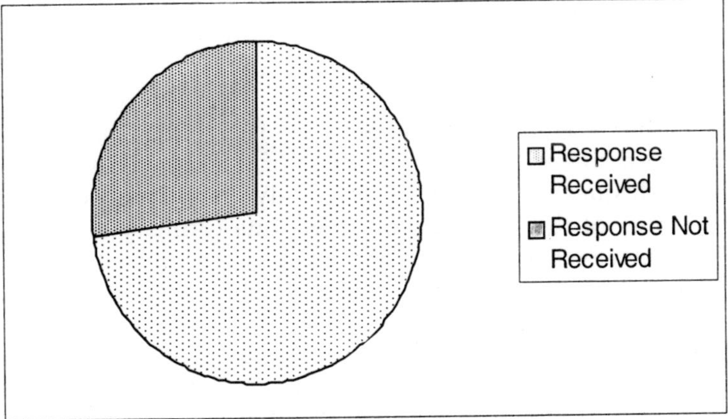

3.5 STATISTICAL TECHNIQUES

The present study being a descriptive, qualitative survey, the researcher has used descriptive analysis and graphical representations wherever necessary. Simple percentage has been calculated at some places.

CHAPTER

4

Analysis and Interpretation of Data

4.0 INTRODUCTION

The present chapter has been devoted to the analysis and interpretation of data in the context of the objectives and the research questions posed in the study. In pursuance of the objectives of the study, the obtained data (Primary as well as Secondary) were tabulated, classified and analysed to yield meaningful interpretation of results, which may eventually lead to significant findings of the study.

The following Table 4.0 gives the Names of the DEIs/OUs selected for the study.

TABLE 4.0

Teacher Education Institutes in India Offering Programmes through Distance Education Mode

Name of the University	*Name of the DEI/OU*
Kakatiya University, Warangal	School of Distance Learning and Continuing Education
S.V. University, Tirupati	Shri Padmavati Mahila Distance Vishvavidyalayam
S.V. University, Tirupati	Directorate of Distance Education

Name of the University	*Name of the DEI/OU*
Andhra University, Vishakhapatnam	School of Distance Learning and Continuing Education
Himachal Pradesh University, Shimla	International Centre for Distance Education and Open Learning
IGNOU, New Delhi	School of Education
Karnataka State Open University, Mysore	Department of Studies and Research in Education
Kota Open University, Kota	School of Education
M.D. University, Rohtak	Department of Distance Education
Punjabi University, Patiala	Department of Correspondence Courses
YCMOU, Nashik	School of Education

In all 11 institutions were administered and responses were received from 8 of them.

No. of Institutes visited for administering Questionnaire	*Response received*	*Response not received*
11	08 (73%)	03 (27%)

TABLE 4.1
Profile of the Institutes/Open Universities

Name of the Distance Education Institute/Open University	*Year of Establishment*	*Affiliated*
1	*2*	*3*
School of Distance Learning and Continuing Education, Kakatiya University, Warangal, Andhra Pradesh	1989	Affiliated To Kakatiya University
Shri Padmavati Mahila Distance Vishvavidyalayam, Tirupathi, Andhra Pradesh	1999	Deemed University,
Directorate of Distance Education, S.V. University, Tirupathi, Andhra Pradesh	1982	S.V. University

1	2	3
School of Distance Learning and Continuing Education, Andhra University, Visakhapatnam, Andhra Pradesh	1972	Andhra University
Deptt. of Education and International Centre for Distance Education and Open Learning, Himachal Pradesh University, Shimla, Himachal Pradesh	1970	H.P. University
School of Education, Indira Gandhi National Open University, New Delhi	1985	IGNOU
Department of Studies and Research in Education, Karnataka State Open University, Mysore, Karnataka	1996	Karnataka State Open University
School of Education, Vardhaman Mahavir Open University, Kota, Rajasthan	1987	V.M. Open University
Department of Distance Education, M.D. University, Rohtak, Haryana	1988	M.D. University
Deptt. of Correspondence Courses, Punjabi University, Patiala, Punjab	1968	Punjabi University
School of Education, Yashwantrao Chavan Maharashtra Open University, Nasik, Maharashtra	1989	YCMOU

4.1 PROFILE OF THE INSTITUTES/OPEN UNIVERSITIES

From the Table 4.1 it is obvious that the oldest of all the institutes is Punjabi University in Patiala, Punjab. It was established in 1968.

The latest one on the scenario is Shri Padmavati Mahila Vishvavidyalayam, Tirupathi in Andhra Pradesh, which was established in 1999 and is a deemed university.

While there were five Institutes conducting teacher education programmes in south, there were equal number of Institutes in the north. YCMOU is the lone University in the west, while there are no University either in the east or even in north-east. While there were quite a number of Universities in this part of the country offering teacher education programmes. All these Universities/institutions discontinued their programmes once NCTE Act came into being and norms and standards were notified for teacher education programme through distance education mode in the Gazette notification of the Government of India.

While there were large number of institutes/universities offering teacher education programme across the country, earlier their operations have been limited with the implementation coming up of NCTE Act in 1995 and more importantly by the Gazette notification of norms and standards for M.Ed. programme through distance education mode in 1999.

We can therefore, conclude that, the handful of Teacher Education Institutes offering courses through distance education mode appears to be serious in their attempt to provide education to the teacher by adhering to the norms and standards as set out by NCTE. It is expected that the programmes offered by these institutes shall have some standards in terms of quality production of study materials as well as in curriculum transaction. These aspects are examined at a later stage.

4.2 PROGRAMMES OFFERED MEDIUM-WISE BY THEIR INTAKE AND PROCEDURE OF ADMISSION

From the Table 4.2 it is seen that institutes like SDLCE, Vishakapatnam in A.P., H.P. University, Shimla, KSOU, Karnataka, Punjabi University, Patiala and YCMOU, Nasik offer both B.Ed. and M.Ed. programmes whereas the rest of the institutes offer only B.Ed. programme.

The enrolment in B.Ed. programmes varies from 250 to 2000 and in the M.Ed. programme from 100 to 475.

The medium of instruction is English and the local vernacular medium like Telugu, Kannada and Marathi in A.P., Karnataka and Maharashtra respectively. In the northern belt it is English and Hindi with the exception of Punjabi University which offers instruction in Punjabi also. Enrolment is on the basis of written tests and interviews for B.Ed. and merit alone for M.Ed. It is seen that regional languages are given the importance. If this is the trend distance education system should be further strengthened so that regional aspirations of the students are taken care.

Of the eleven universities offering teacher education programme through distance education mode in the entire

TABLE 4.2

Programme Offered Medium-wise by their Intake and Procedure of Admission

Name of the Distance Education Institute/ Open University	*Name of Programmes*	*Total No. of Seats*	*Medium of Instruction*	*Enrolment Procedure*
School of Distance Learning and Continuing Education, Kakatiya University, Warangal, Andhra Pradesh	B.Ed.	500 Co-Ed	English	
Shri Padmavati Mahila Distance Vishvavidyalayam, Tirupathi, Andhra Pradesh	B.Ed.	500 Girls only	English	
Directorate of Distance Education, S.V. University, Tirupathi, Andhra Pradesh	B.Ed.	500 Co-Ed	English	
School of Distance Learning and Continuing Education, Andhra University, Visakhapatnam, Andhra Pradesh	B.Ed. M.Ed.	750 100 Co-Ed.	English/Telugu	
Department of Education and International Centre for Distance Education and Open Learning, Himachal Pradesh University, Shimla, Himachal Pradesh	B.Ed. M.Ed.	450 250 Co-Ed.	Hindi Hindi	
School of Education, Indira Gandhi National Open University, New Delhi	B.Ed. DPE	2000 1200 Co-Ed.	English English	Written Test

Department of Studies and Research in Education Karnataka State Open University, Mysore, Karnataka	B.Ed. M.Ed.	500 475 Co-Ed.	English/Karnataka English/Karnataka	Written Test Merit alone
School of Education, Vardhaman Mahavir Open University, Kota, Rajasthan	B.Ed.	500 Co-Ed.	Hindi	
Department of Distance Education, M.D. University, Rohtak, Haryana	B.Ed.	250 Co-Ed.	English/Hindi	
Department of Correspondence Courses, Punjabi University, Patiala, Punjab	B.Ed. M.Ed.	400 250 Co-Ed.	Hindi/Punjabi/ English	
School of Education, Yashwantrao Chavan Maharashtra Open University, Nasik, Maharashtra	B.Ed. M.Ed.	1500 250 Co-Ed.	Marathi	Interviews Merit

country only five universities are offering M.Ed. programmes with a total enrolment of about 1325 students only. As against this, if we see the enrolment figure of M.Ed. programme in the traditional face to face set-up, there are approximately 165 students enrolled in M.Ed. programme in the conventional universities of Maharashtra State. This comes to roughly per cent of the regular enrolment. However, none of the institutes/Universities offered M.Ed. programme singularly, although there are instances of institutes/universities offering B.Ed. programme alone. Why are the institutes/universities offerings B.Ed. and M.Ed. programme together or singly only the B.Ed. programmes. Is it not viable to offer M.Ed. programme alone or there are no takers? What does this trend indicate? Don't we need more and more number of candidates upgrade their qualification by enrolling in M.Ed. programme through distance education mode? What is the requirement of manpower at the level of M.Ed.? As far as the researcher's knowledge goes in the state of Maharashtra, there is a great demand for M.Ed. programme through distance education mode since the Maharashtra Government stipulates that all those teachers in junior colleges need to have M.Ed./M.Phil. in order to be considered for promotion in the next scale after their initial induction into teaching profession.

Since B.Ed. programme is offered by all the Universities, it appears to be the popular and perhaps most demanding programme by the students. That could be the reason why the NCTE came out with norms and standards for B.Ed. programme through distance education mode much earlier than that of M.Ed. programme which came as late as in 1999 after nearly four years of the establishment of NCTE.

4.3 QUALIFICATIONS AND EXPERIENCE OF FACULTY

From the Table 4.3 it is seen that faculty strength varies from minimum 4 in Kakatiya University, to a maximum of 23 in H.P. University, Shimla. Most of the faculty members have a doctorate degree to their credit and are generally highly experienced.

The number of faculty members in Himachal Pradesh University is higher because the University conducts both regular and distance education mode teacher training programme. It can be inferred that at the insistence of NCTE, the university/institutes

Figure 4.1: Bar Graph Showing Intake of B.Ed. and M.Ed. Programme

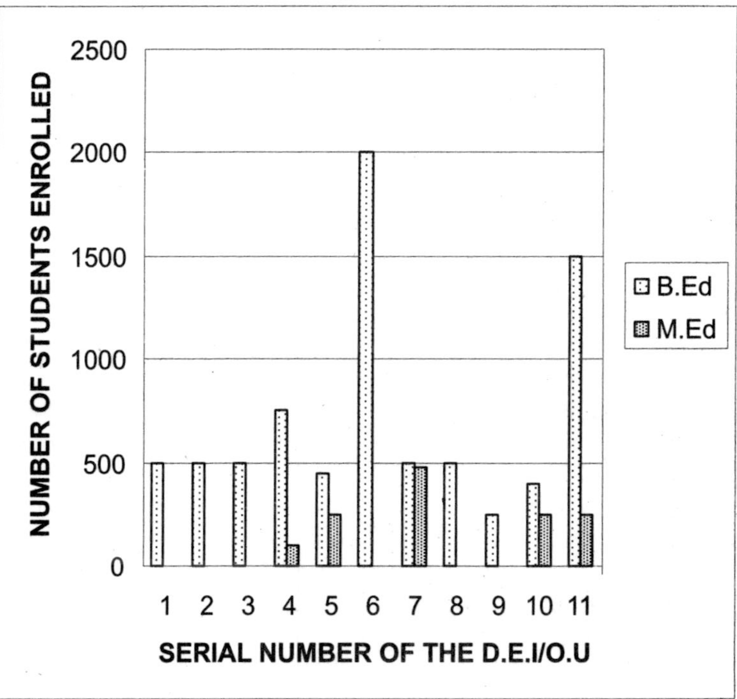

Key:

Sl. No.	*Name of the Distance Education Institute/Open University*
1.	School of Distance Learning and Continuing Education, Kakatiya University, Warangal, Andhra Pradesh.
2.	Shri Padmavati Mahila Distance Vishvavidyalayam, Tirupathi, Andhra Pradesh.
3.	Directorate of Distance Education, S.V. University, Tirupathi, Andhra Pradesh.
4.	School of Distance Learning and Continuing Education, Andhra University, Visakhapatnam, Andhra Pradesh.
5.	Department of Education and International Centre for Distance Education and Open Learning, Himachal Pradesh University, Shimla, Himachal Pradesh.
6.	School of Education, Indira Gandhi National Open University, New Delhi
7.	Department of Studies and Research in Education, Karnataka State Open University, Mysore, Karnataka.
8.	School of Education, Vardhaman Mahavir Open University, Kota, Rajasthan.
9.	Department of Distance Education, M.D. University, Rohtak, Haryana.
10.	Department of Correspondence Courses, Punjabi University, Patiala, Punjab.
11.	School of Education, Yashwantrao Chavan Maharashtra Open University, Nasik, Maharashtra.

TABLE 4.3

Qualification and Experience of Faculty

Name of the Distance Education Institute/ Open University	*Total No. of Faculty Members*	*No. of Faculty with Ph.D.*	*Teaching Experience*		
			1-10 yrs.	*11-20 yrs.*	*21-30 yrs.*
School of Distance Learning and Continuing Education, Kakatiya University, Warangal, Andhra Pradesh	4				
Shri Padmavati Mahila Distance Vishvavidyalayam, Tirupathi, Andhra Pradesh	8				
Directorate of Distance Education, S.V. University, Tirupathi, Andhra Pradesh	10				
School of Distance Learning and Continuing Education, Andhra University, Visakhapatnam, Andhra Pradesh	4	4			
Department of Education and International Centre for Distance Education and Open Learning, Himachal Pradesh University, Shimla, Himachal Pradesh	23				

School of Education, Indira Gandhi National Open University, New Delhi	13	4			
Department of Studies and Research in Education, Karnataka State Open University, Mysore, Karnataka	13	7			
School of Education, Vardhaman Mahavir Open University, Kota, Rajasthan	4	4	5	3	5
Department of Distance Education, M.D. University, Rohtak, Haryana					
Department of Correspondence Courses, Punjabi University, Patiala, Punjab	4	4			5
School of Education, Yashwantrao Chavan Maharashtra Open University, Nasik, Maharashtra	10	6	5	1	4

offering teacher education programmes are appointing core faculty members to over see the curriculum transaction and of course maintaining quality of study material and instruction.

Figure 4.2: Bar Graph Showing Faculty Strength and Qualification

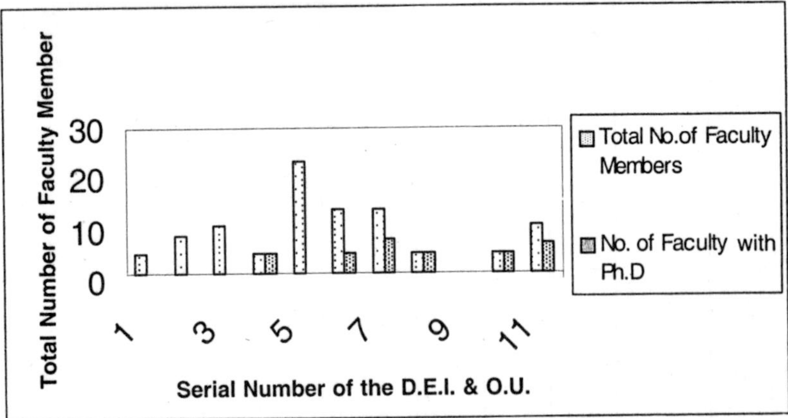

Key:

Sl. No.	Name of the Distance Education Institute/Open University
1.	School of Distance Learning and Continuing Education, Kakatiya University, Warangal, Andhra Pradesh.
2.	Shri Padmavati Mahila Distance Vishvavidyalayam, Tirupathi, Andhra Pradesh.
3.	Directorate of Distance Education, S.V. University, Tirupathi, Andhra Pradesh.
4.	School of Distance Learning and Continuing Education, Andhra University, Visakhapatnam, Andhra Pradesh.
5.	Department of Education and International Centre for Distance Education and Open Learning, Himachal Pradesh University, Shimla, Himachal Pradesh.
6.	School of Education, Indira Gandhi National Open University, New Delhi.
7.	Department of Studies and Research in Education, Karnataka State Open University, Mysore, Karnataka.
8.	School of Education, Vardhaman Mahavir Open University, Kota, Rajasthan.
9.	Department of Distance Education, M.D. University, Rohtak, Haryana.
10.	Department of Correspondence Courses, Punjabi University, Patiala, Punjab.
11.	School of Education, Yashwantrao Chavan Maharashtra Open University, Nasik, Maharashtra.

TABLE 4.4

Description of Study Materials

Name of the Distance Education Institute/ Open University	*Format*	*Supplimentary Materials*	*Size*	*Topic Coverage*	*Language*	*Bibliography*
Dept. of Education and International Centre for Distance Education and Open Learning, Himachal Pradesh University, Shimla, Himachal Pradesh	SIM		>200PP	Adequate	Simple	Adequate
Department of Studies and Research in Education, Karnataka State Open University, Mysore, Karnataka	SIM		>200PP	Adequate	Simple	Adequate
School of Education, Vardhaman Mahavir Open University, Kota, Rajasthan	Printed Booklet	Films, CALs	>200PP	Adequate	Simple	Adequate
Department of Correspondence Courses, Punjabi University, Patiala, Punjab.	Printed Booklet Topic-wise Notes	CALs	>200PP	Adequate	Simple	Adequate
School of Education, Yashwantrao Chavan Maharashtra Open University, Nasik, Maharashtra	SIM	A.V.A. Audio Cassettes	100-150P	Adequate	Simple	Adequate

4.4 DESCRIPTION OF STUDY MATERIALS

From the Table 4.4 it is clear that study materials are either in the SIM format, printed booklets or topic-wise notes. They are supplemented by Films, A.V. Aids, Audio cassettes and Computer Assisted Lessons. The size of the study material is usually around 200 pages, written in simple language with adequate topic coverage and bibliography.

The study materials of all the four Open Universities offering teacher education programme through distance education mode are structured in self-instructional format. The size of the booklet is in A/4 size paper and each course is divided into some blocks for easy handling so that it does not unnecessarily become bulky. Some units constitute a block. Each unit normally consists of 8 to 10 printed pages.

The study material of YCMOU, KSOU and KOU are in Marathi, Kannada and Hindi languages respectively, while the study material of IGNOU is in English only.

The study materials of distance education institutes were procured for analysis. It was found that the study material of SDLCE, Andhra University, were in line with the study material of Open University, i.e. prepared in self-instructional material format. The cover page is multi-coloured with relevant pictures on the subject as per requirement. The syllabus of each paper is provided in the study material for easy reference of the students followed by contents. Each unit of the study material is divided into smaller sub-units containing paragraphs with the important points being highlighted. Wherever required, pictures, photographs, graphics, illustrations are also provided for better understanding. Check your progress is also given at the end of each sub-unit with adequate space for writing the answers. *Each unit contains structure, introduction, objective, contents, check your progress, let's sum up, glossary, unit-end activity, recommended books for reading and answers to check your progress.*

The study material is also supplemented by syllabus and model question papers, which has been printed separately and is being distributed to the students. The question papers are in bilingual.

At Sri Padmavati Mahila Vishwavidyalayam, and S.V.

University's Directorate of Distance Education, they are having study materials in the regional language, i.e. Telugu.

The study material of ICEDOL of H.P. University is not strictly as per the self-instruction material format but fairly comprehensive with objectives of the unit, illustration and suggested readings at the end of each unit.

4.5 PREPARATION OF STUDY MATERIAL

Preparation of study material is an important activity in the distance education system. It is important to know how the study material is developed and who are involved in the process of developing study material for different learners as study material is the main stay in this system.

From the Table 4.5 it is seen that in Open Universities study materials are developed by a course term comprising subjects experts, language editor, educational technologist and media expert. Evaluation of study material is done periodically by experts and after getting feedback from students, it is done in relation to the relevance of content, style of presentation and language difficulty. The booklets are in paperback with standard quality paper and printing

In the DEI it is observed that subject experts and staff members of DEI prepare the study material. Again, the study material is evaluated by experts with relation to relevance of content, style of presentation and language difficulty. In DCC in Punjabi University the study materials are printed in good quality paper but just stapled, whereas in DEI like SDLCE of Andhra University, they are also bound in paperback with colorful cover page.

Thus we can conclude that the course materials are prepared in general by a course team, are evaluated by experts in the field of teacher education and distance education in relation to the relevance of content, style of presentation and language difficulty. Generally they are good paper bound. Booklets and their cost is included in the course fees.

In both Open Universities and DEI's the cost of the study material is included in the fee and students are not charged separately.

TABLE 4.5

Preparation of Study Material

Name of the Distance Education Institute/ Open University	*Prepared by*	*Evaluation*		*External Aspects*	*Cost*
		With reference to	*Done By*		
Department of Studies and Research in Education Karnataka State Open University, Mysore, Karnataka	Course Team	Relevance and Style	Experts	V. Good, Hard Bound	Incl. in Fees
School of Education, Vardhaman Mahavir Open University, Kota, Rajasthan	Course Team	Language Difficulty	Student, Course Writs	Good Hard Bound	Incl. in Fees
Department of Correspondence Courses, Punjabi University, Patiala, Punjab	Staff, Sub. Experts	Relevance of Content	Experts	Just Stapled	Incl. in Fees
School of Education, Yashwantrao Chavan Maharashtra Open University, Nasik, Maharashtra	Course Team, Staff of Study Centers	Relevance and Style Language difficulty	Experts	Good Hard Bound	Incl. in Fees

TABLE 4.6

Conduct of Practice Teaching

Name of the Distance Education Institute/ Open University	*Schedule of Practice Teaching*	*No. of Lessons*	*Guidance Type*	*Evaluation Done by*	*Feedback to students*
Department of Studies and Research in Education Karnataka State Open University, Mysore, Karnataka	During the Course	40	Group only	Teacher Educator	Group
School of Education, Vardhaman Mahavir Open University, Kota, Rajasthan	During the Course	40	Individual and Group	Principal, Teacher Educator, Core Staff	Individual and Group
Department of Correspondence Courses, Punjabi University, Patiala, Punjab	During the Course	40	Individual and Group	Core Staff of DEI	Individual and Group
School of Education, Yashwantrao Chavan Maharashtra Open University, Nasik, Maharashtra	During the Course	40	Individual only	Teacher Educator, School Teacher	Individual and Group

4.6 CONDUCT OF PRACTICE TEACHING

Conduct of practice teaching is one of the very important component of teacher education programme precisely because of this component, it was believed that teacher education programme cannot be delivered effectively through distance education mode as it could be through face to face classroom teaching. Table 4.6 shows how practice teaching is being conducted through distance education mode in Indian universities.

From the Table 4.6 it is seen that as far as practice teaching goes, all the institutes insist on giving 40 lessons during the programme (20 in each method). Lesson guidance is given both individually and in groups. The lessons are evaluated by teacher educators, school teachers, principals of schools and core staff of DEIs. The students are given feedback both individually and in groups.

It was found that delivery of lessons in the schools was made compulsory in the institutes offering teacher education programmes. Even as many as 40 lessons were delivered by each student.

It appears that, these lessons delivered by the student in the practicing schools were in no way less rigorous as in case of regular teaching leaving no scope for doubts of any kind that practicals could not be conducted through distance education mode. It is in fact made possible through collaborations with schools, in the nearby areas. Moreover, the candidates enrolled for distance education programmes are already teachers in schools/ Junior colleges and they have a minimum of 2 years of teaching experience to their credit before they took admission for the said programme.

4.7 ORGANISATION OF PERSONAL CONTACT PROGRAMME

In order to remove isolation of the teachers and to have better coordination/contact with other colleagues, P.C.P. lectures are organised during summer vacation/winter vacation/Christmas vacation. During the PCP the students get an opportunity to not only interact with themselves but with their teachers to solve their problems/difficulties if any.

TABLE 4.7

Organisation of Personal Contact Programme Lectures

Name of the Distance Education Institute/ Open University	*Duration of PCP*	*Nature of Participant*	*Venue of PCP*	*Staff engaged in PCP*
School of Education, Indira Gandhi National Open University, New Delhi	Given Time Slot	Compulsory	Study Centre	DEI, Visiting
Department of Studies and Research in Education, Karnataka State Open University, Mysore, Karnataka	6 hrs	Compulsory	Study Centre	DEI, Visiting
Department of Distance Education, M.D. University, Rohtak, Haryana	Min. 7 Days	Compulsory	DEI	DEI Visiting
Department of Correspondence Courses, Punjabi University, Patiala, Punjab	Given Time Slot	Compulsory	DEI Contact Centre	DEI Staff

The PCPs are held in varying times depending on the institutes either at the beginning or at the end or in the middle of the course. The duration is usually given time slot, which may range from 6 hours to a maximum of 7 days.

The attendance is compulsory. These programmes are conducted at the contact centers, study centers or DEIs. The faculty members involved are the staff of the DEIs, visiting faculty or both.

TABLE 4.8

Support Services

Name of the Distance Education Institute/ Open University	*Library*	*Other Facilities*
School of Education, Indira Gandhi National Open University, New Delhi	Refernce, Lending	Radio counseling
Department of Studies and Research in Education, Karnataka State Open University, Mysore, Karnataka	Refernce, Lending	Study Room, Photo Copying
School of Education, Vardhaman Mahavir Open University, Kota, Rajasthan	Refernce, Lending	Photo Copying
Department of Correspondence Courses, Punjabi University, Patiala, Punjab	Refernce, Lending	
School of Education, Yashwantrao Chavan Maharashtra Open University, Nasik, Maharashtra	Refernce, Lending	A.V. Aids, On-line Guidance

4.8 SUPPORT SERVICES

In distance education system, support services are important for many reasons as it can enhance enrolment, decrease dropout and contribute to academic success by breaking the barrier of isolation. To what extent support services is an integral part of the delivery of quality distance education programmes especially in a professional subject like teacher education is shown in Table 4.8.

From the above table it is seen that the support services

provided include library with reference and lending facilities, study rooms, photocopying facilities, audio-visual aids, etc. In YCMOU, on line guidance is also given. Certainly if these facilities are used by the students effectively, it will enhance their understanding the subject matter which will help in getting through in the examination attributing higher completion/success rate. But unfortunately the study could not ascertain the views of the students about the services provided. This is one of the limitations of this study. However, YCMOU goes a step further in enhancing the support services provided to its teacher trainees by on line service.

It is precisely for this reason the distance education institutes and open universities plan student support service in the form of regional services division/student support services center.

If one looks at the Table 4.8 closely, it can be observed that the OUs have well structured system of student support services, while the distance education institutes are yet to catch up the trend. It is therefore, suggested that the distance education institute in the conventional system should strengthen the student support services by making adequate provision in that regard.

TABLE 4.9

Areas of Counselling

Name of the Distance Education Institute/Open University	*Areas of Counselling*
Department of Studies and Research in Education, Karnataka State Open University, Mysore, Karnataka	Choice of Papers, Practice Teaching
School of Education, Vardhaman Mahavir Open University, Kota, Rajasthan	As per students'demand
Deptt. of Correspondence Courses, Punjabi University, Patiala, Punjab	Practice Teaching, Use of Library, Examination
School of Education, Yashwantrao Chavan Maharashtra Open University, Nasik, Maharashtra	Choice of Papers, Practice Teaching, Confidence Building, Examination

4.9 AREAS OF COUNSELLING

The counseling is the most important but often neglected activity in any distance education programme. Unlike the conventional mode where students have instant and constant access to teachers, in the distance education mode counselling at various stages in the programme like admission, assignments, personal guidance, etc. acts as a buffer to reduce the psychological stress and anxiety of the students.

From the above Table 4.9 it is seen that the counselling is given as per the student's demand regarding choice of papers, practice teaching, use of library, examination, confidence building, etc.

4.10 EVALUATION OF TERM END EXAM.

Evaluation is an on going process with 25% to 30% weightage being given to internals. It is usually done through assignments, oral and written tests, seminars and external examination. Remaining 75% to 70% weightage is being given to term end examination/final examination. Evaluation is continuous in both distance education institute and open universities. Students submit assignments which is compulsory and at the end, appear at the term end final examination. This is revealed in Table 4.10.

4.11 ASSIGNMENT AND IT'S PURPOSE

The purpose of introducing assignment in distance education mode is to ensure continuous assessment of student's performance and giving feedback to the student for improvement. In a way, the assignment serves the purpose of teaching at a distance through tutor comments on the assignment which are written individually/personally pointing out the individual mistakes. Moreover submission of assignments is not only helpful in clarifying the concept but also helps in improving the performance of the students in the final/term end examination.

It is observed from the Table 4.11 that assignments are compulsory in all units and for all students. Their main purpose is for student support and assessment. The students are required to submit assignments of 6-10 pages in each unit. They are

TABLE 4.10

Evaluation of Term End Exam.

Name of the Distance Education Institute/ Open University	*Total Marks In./Ext.*	*Int. Ext./ Only Ext.*	*Min. Passing marks Th./Practical*	*Nature of Evaluation*	*Tools Used*
Department of Studies and Research in Education, Karnataka State Open University, Mysore, Karnataka	25%/75% 1500 (900+600)	Both	380/220	Continuous Evaluation	Assn., Int. Test, Exam.
School of Education, Vardhaman Mahavir Open University, Kota, Rajasthan	30%/70%	Both	40/60	On-going	Assn., Seminars, Exam.
Department of Correspondence Courses, Punjabi University, Patiala, Punjab				On-going	Assn., Int. Test, Exam.
School of Education, Yashwantrao Chavan Maharashtra Open University, Nasik, Maharashtra	1000 (500+500)	Both		On-going CGPA Done	Assn., Int. Test, Orals, Exam.

TABLE 4.11

Assignments and their Purpose

Name of the Distance Education Institute/ Open Universit	*Nature of assignment submission*	*Length of assignment*	*Time given for assignment submission*	*Evaluation of assignment*
Department of Studies and Research in Education, Karnataka State Open University, Mysore, Karnataka	Compulsory in all units	11-20 pages each		Evaluated by staff of DEI, Individual comments and Marks added to the final
School of Education, Vardhaman Mahavir Open University, Kota, Rajasthan	Compulsory in all units	6-10 pages each	3 months	Evaluated by part time tutor, Individual comments and Marks added to the final
Department of Correspondence Courses, Punjabi University, Patiala, Punjab	Compulsory in all units	6-10 pages each	15 days	Evaluated by staff of DEI, Individual comments and Marks added to the final
School of Education, Yashwantrao Chavan Maharashtra Open University, Nasik, Maharashtra	Compulsory in all units	6-10 pages each	6 months	Evaluated by staff of DEI, Individual comments and Marks added to the final

evaluated by staff of DEI or part time tutors. The comments given are usually individualistic in nature. The time given for submission ranges from 15 days to 6 months. The marks of these assignments are added to the final examination marks.

4.12 MAJOR FINDINGS

The following are the major findings of the present research study.

Although the number of teacher education institutes offering teacher education programmes through distance education mode was quite large before the NCTE act was implemented in 1995, presently the teacher education programme through the distance mode are offered in 11 NCTE approved distance education institutes and open universities in the entire country.

The oldest of all the institutes is Punjabi University in Patiala, Punjab which was established in 1968. The latest one on the scenario is Shri Padmavati Mahila Vishvavidyalayam, Tirupathi in Andhra Pradesh, which was established in 1999 and is a deemed university. It is important to note that these programmes are offered only for in-service teachers.

Institutes like Andhra University, Vishakapatnam, H.P. University, Shimla; KSOU, Karnataka; Punjabi University, Patiala and YCMOU, Nasik offer both B.Ed. and M.Ed. programmes whereas the rest of the institutions offer only B.Ed. programme. The enrolment in B.Ed. course varies from 250 to 2000 and in the M.Ed. course from 100 to 475. The higher enrolment figures is in respect of open university only, whose jurisdiction covers the entire country in case of IGNOU and the entire state in case of state open universities like Karnataka and Rajasthan.

The medium of instruction is English and the local vernacular medium like Telugu, Kannada and Marathi in A.P., Karnataka and Maharashtra respectively. In the northern belt it is English and Hindi with the exception of Punjabi University which offers instruction in Punjabi also. Enrolment is on the basis of written tests and interviews for B.Ed. and merit alone for M.Ed. In some cases weightage is given to those teachers who are having longer teaching experience in school systems.

The faculty strength varies from a minimum of 4 in Kakatiya University, to a maximum of 23 in Himachal Pradesh University,

Shimla. It is a good trend that all the institutions running programme through distance education mode are at least having some core faculty member to oversee the programme delivery of the course. Most of the faculty members have a doctorate degree to their credit and are generally highly experienced.

The course materials are prepred in the SIM form in case of OU and printed booklets or topic-wise notes are supplied by distance education institute. They are supplemented by Films, Audio Visual Aids, Audio Cassettes and Computer Assisted Lessons. The size of SIM is usually around 200 pages, written in simple language with adequate topic coverage and bibliography.

Such is the quality of study materials of IGNOU and YCMOU that they have bagged international awards from organisation such as COL Canada for its quality of material production. In fact both the teachers and students of conventional university use the study materials of distance education programmes to supplement their classroom teaching and learning.

The course materials are prepared in general by a course team, are evaluated by experts in the field of teacher education and distance education in relation to the relevance of content, style of presentation and language difficulty. Generally they are good hard bound booklets and their cost is included in the course fees.

As far as practice teaching goes, all the institutions insist on giving 40 lessons during the course (20 in each method). Lesson guidance is given both individually and in groups. The lessons are evaluated by teacher educators, school teachers, principals of schools and core staff of DEIs. The students are given feedback both individually and in groups.

The Personal Contact Programme lectures are held in varying times depending on the institutions either at the beginning or at the end or in the middle of the course. The duration of PCP is usually a given time slot, which range from 6 days to a maximum of 15 days. The attendance is compulsory. These programmes are conducted at the contact centers, study centers or DEIs. The faculty members involved are the staff of the DEIs, visiting faculty or both.

It is also seen that the support services provided include library with reference and lending facilities, study rooms, photocopying facilities, audio-visual aids. In YCMOU, on line guidance is also given.

The counselling is given as per the student's demand regarding choice of papers, practice teaching, use of library, examination, confidence building, etc.

Evaluation is an ongoing on process with 25 to 30 per cent weightage being given to internal. It is usually done through assignments, oral and written tests, seminars and external examination. Remaining 70-75 per cent weightage is being given to term end examination/final examination. Evaluation is continuous in both distance education institute and OUs.

Assignments are compulsory for all students. Their main purpose is to enhance student learning and assessment of their performance midway. The students are required to submit assignments of 6-10 pages in each unit. Staff of DEI or part time tutors evaluates the assignment. The comments given are usually individualistic in nature. The time given for submission ranges from 15 days to 6 months. The marks of these assignments are added to the final examination marks. From the above findings it is obvious that all the distance education institutes and open universities are adhering to the NCTE norms.

CHAPTER

5

Summary and Conclusions

5.0 INTRODUCTION

In a democracy committed to the goal of education for all and cent per cent literacy rate, the need for good teachers is self-evident. The ever increasing student enrolment at all stages of education calls for a steady supply of well trained teachers, a demand, which the conventional teacher training institutions are unable to cope with. Here the importance of offering teacher education through the distance mode steps in. There are a number of dual mode universities, operating through DEIs and single mode universities called as OUs in India, offering teacher education programmes through the distance education mode.

Since the quality of these programmes is debatable, hence the NCTE has laid down some guidelines for these programmes. The present study is focused on only such institutions that are providing teacher education courses by adhering to the NCTE norms and are recognised by NCTE and UGC.

5.1 SUMMARY

With this background in view, the present study is aimed at looking into the teacher education programmes through distance education mode in Indian universities. In all 11 institutions approved by NCTE conducting B.Ed. and M.Ed. programmes have been considered for this study. The following table gives the list of OUs and DEIs chosen for the study.

TABLE 5.1

Distance Education Institues/Open Universities Selected for the Study

Name of the Distance Education Institute/ Open University	*Affiliated to*
School of Distance Learning and Continuing Education, Kakatiya University, Warrangal, Andhra Pradesh	Kakatiya University
Shri Padmavati Mahila Distance Vishvavidyalayam, Tirupathi, Andhra Pradesh	Deemed University
Directorate of Distance Education, S.V. University, Tirupathi, Andhra Pradesh	S.V. University
School of Distance Learning and Continuing Education, Andhra University, Visakhapatnam, Andhra Pradesh	Andhra University
Department of Education and International Centre for Distance Education and Open Learning, Himachal Pradesh University, Shimla, Himachal Pradesh	H.P. University
School of Education, Indira Gandhi National Open University, New Delhi	IGNOU
Department of Studies and Research in Education Karnataka State Open University, Mysore, Karnataka	Karnataka State Open University
School of Education, Vardhaman Mahavir Open University, Kota, Rajasthan	V.M. Open University
Department of Distance Education, M.D. University, Rohtak, Haryana	M.D. University
Department of Correspondence Courses, Punjabi University, Patiala, Punjab	Punjabi University
School of Education, Yashwantrao Chavan Maharashtra Open University, Nasik, Maharashtra	YCMOU

Statement of the Problem

The problem under investigation is entitled "A study of teacher education programmes offered through distance education mode in Indian universities."

Aims of the Study

As the present study attempts to analyse and evaluate the details of programme delivery of Teacher Education Programmes at the all India level, the study will primarily look into the existing system of :

1. Organisation of Personal contact programme, i.e. Duration of the programme, contents covered, background of tèachers engaged in teaching, etc.
2. Course material, i.e. size/volume of the course materials, whether written in self-instructional style with self-check exercises, etc.
3. Response sheet, i.e. evaluation of response sheets whether comments are written/marks awarded, size of the response sheets, whether compulsory or optional, essay type questions or short answer objective type questions, etc.
4. Practice Teaching, i.e. number of lessons to be practised, method of supervision, practicing school, etc.
5. Based upon the findings of this study, policy implications will be suggested to effectively deliver the programme.

Objectives of the Study

The specific objectives of the study are as follows:

1. To examine printed course materials, coverage and the media combined packages used.
2. To study the organization of personal contact programmes for the conduct of lectures and practice teaching lessons.
3. To find out the process of evaluation of response sheets.
4. To suggest measures for improving the programme delivery of Teacher Education courses.

Methodology

The present study is a census survey of the descriptive, qualitative type, describing and interpreting what is.

The word "survey" means to view comprehensively and in detail. In another sense it refers specifically to the act of "obtaining data for mapping". The term survey is generally used for the type of research which proposes to ascertain what is the normal or typical condition or practice at the present time. What is distinctive about the survey is its combination of a commitment to a breadth of study, a focus on the snapshot at a given point of time and a dependence on empirical data.

The survey involves a clearly defined problem and definite objective. It requires expert and imaginative planning, careful analysis and interpretation of the data gathered and logical and skillful reporting of the findings.

In order to achieve the objectives of the present study, census survey method of descriptive, qualitative type was used as this was found to be the most appropriate method to study the programmes of Teacher Education offered through distance education mode in Indian universities.

In this study the researcher has:

1. Identified the various NCTE approved OUs and DEIs offering Teacher Education programme through distance education mode.
2. Described the profile of the various selected institutions in detail.
3. Analysed and interpreted the available data qualitatively.

Sample

Being a census study all the NCTE approved OUs and DEIs in India, conducting teacher education programmes were considered.

5.2 MAJOR FINDINGS

The following are the major findings of the present research study.

Although the number of teacher education institutes offering teacher education programmes through distance education mode was quite large before the NCTE act was implemented in 1995, presently the teacher education programme through the distance mode are offered in 11 NCTE approved distance education institutes and open universities in the entire country.

The oldest of all the institutes is Punjabi University in Patiala, Punjab which was established in 1968. The latest one on the scenario is Shri Padmavati Mahila Vishvavidyalayam, Tirupathi in Andhra Pradesh, which was established in 1999 and is a deemed university. It is important to note that these programmes are offered only for in-service teachers.

Institutes like SDLCE, Vishakhapatnam in A.P., H.P. University, Shimla; KSOU, Karnataka; Punjabi University, Patiala and YCMOU, Nasik offer both B.Ed. and M.Ed. programmes whereas the rest of the institutions offer only B.Ed. programme. The enrolment in B.Ed. course varies from 250 to 2000 and in the M.Ed. course from 100 to 475. The higher enrolment figures is in respect of open university only, whose jurisdiction covers the entire country in case of IGNOU and the entire state in case of state open universities like Karnataka and Rajasthan.

The medium of instruction is English and the local vernacular medium like Telugu, Kannada and Marathi in A.P., Karnataka and Maharashtra respectively. In the northern belt it is English and Hindi with the exception of Punjabi University, which offers instruction in Punjabi also. Enrolment is on the basis of written tests and interviews for B.Ed. and merit alone for M.Ed. In some cases weightage is given to those teachers who are having longer teaching experience in school systems.

The faculty strength varies from a minimum of 4 in Kakatiya University, to a maximum of 23 in Himachal Pradesh University. It is a good trend that all the institutions running programme through distance education mode are at least having some core faculty member to oversee the programme delivery of the course. Most of the faculty members have a doctorate degree to their credit and are generally highly experienced.

The course materials are prepared in the SIM form in case of OU and printed booklets or distance education institutes supply topic-wise notes. They are supplemented by Films, Audio Visual Aids, Audio Cassettes and Computer Assisted Lessons. The size of SIM is usually around 200 pages, written in simple language with adequate topic coverage and bibliography.

Such is quality of study material's of IGNOU and YCMOU that they have bagged international awards and recognition from organisation such as COL Canada for its quality of material production. In fact both the teachers and students of conventional university use the study materials of distance education programme to supplement their classroom teaching and learning.

The course materials are prepared in general by a course team, are evaluated by experts in the field of teacher education and distance education in relation to the relevance of content, style of presentation and language difficulty. Generally they are good hard bound booklets and their cost is included in the course fees.

As far as practice teaching goes, all the institutions insist on giving 40 lessons during the course (20 in each method). Lesson guidance is given both individually and in groups. The lessons are evaluated by teacher educators, school teachers, principals of schools and core staff of DEIs. The students are given feedback both individually and in groups.

The Personal Contact Programme lectures are held in varying times depending on the institutions either at the beginning or at the end or in the middle of the course. The duration of PCP is usually a given time slot, which range from 6 days to a maximum of 15 days. The attendance is compulsory. These programmes are conducted at the contact centers, study centers or DEIs. The faculty members involved are the staff of the DEIs, visiting faculty or both.

It is also seen that the support services provided include library with reference and lending facilities, study rooms, photocopying facilities, audio-visual aids. In YCMOU, on-line guidance is also given.

The counselling is given as per the student's demand regarding choice of papers, practice teaching, use of library, examination, confidence building, etc.

Evaluation is an ongoing process with 25 to 30 per cent weightage being given to internal. It is usually done through assignments, oral and written tests, seminars and external examination. Remaining 70-75 per cent weightage is being given to term end examination/final examination. Evaluation is continuous in both distance education institute and OUs.

Assignments are compulsory for all students. Their main purpose is to enhance student learning and assessment of their performance midway. The students are required to submit assignments of 6-10 pages in each unit. Staff of DEI or part time tutors evaluates the assignment. The comments given are usually individualistic in nature. The time given for submission ranges from 15 days to 6 months. The marks of these assignments are added to the final examination marks. From the above findings it is obvious that all the distance education institutes and open universities adhere to the NCTE norms.

5.3 SUGGESTIONS FOR FURTHER RESEARCH

As research in the alternative modes of teacher education requires longitudinal studies, researches based on a sound conceptual framework of teacher education can be conceived, designed and implemented. Following are some of the relatively unprobed areas:

1. In-depth studies of teacher education institutions, training situation and teachers at the micro level could be conducted to discover new variables for improving effectiveness of teacher trainees and for explaining the results emerging from macro analysis of the studies.
2. Impact studies of the NCTE's norms and standards, its role as a regulatory body on teacher education institution could be conducted.
3. A comparative study of teacher education programme offered by private managements and distance education mode could be made to findout the effectiveness of delivery of the programme.
4. Effectiveness of teacher education programme through distance education mode on student's performance and retention rate can be studied.
5. A comparative study of teacher education programmes offered by single mode OUs and dual mode distance education institute could be undertaken to study the impact of technology used in the programme delivery. Similar kind of comparative study could be conducted

between conventional University and Open University to study the impact of face to face component of teaching.

5.4 POLICY IMPLICATIONS

As the study reveals that there are hardly any DEIs/OUs in the east or north-east offering teacher education programmes through distance education mode, it would be welcome idea if efforts are taken in that direction. It is good to note that recently four NCTE recognized institutions have started B.Ed. programme through distance education mode.

The findings of this project vindicates the report given by R.C. Das Committee appointed by NCTE on part time teacher education programme. Therefore, as a policy decision distance education system should be encouraged to offer teacher education courses as it is an equally effective, efficient and viable mode.

Moreover, the DEIs of the conventional universities should be encouraged to offer teacher education programmes through distance education mode as this has proved to be equally effective in delivery of the programme.

Conclusion

The research shows that distance education, in its various forms can work and if well designed can be educationally effective. It has been applied to the education of teachers and has been shown to be effective on a number of measures. Earlier studies have indicated that distance education programmes have often shown advantages over conventional programmes.

Distance education has been used to teach, support and develop teachers for many years. Since the NCERT started the summer training programme for the in-service teachers during the 1960s, the same mode could still be used for imparting teacher education programme through distance education mode more effectively now with the availability of new technology.

APPENDIX I

The Organization of Teacher Training at a Distance with Particular Reference to Kenya

Peter E. Kinyanjui

Context

Many countries have used distance education for teacher training. This article focuses on such programs in Kenya. Please note that the full text of this book is available to those with adequate computer capacity at the following URL: http://imagebank2.worldbank.org/

Source

Kinyanjui, Peter E., "The Organization of Teacher Training at a Distance with Particular Reference to Kenya." In Paud Murphy and Abdelwahed Zhiri, eds., *Distance Education in Anglophone Africa: Experience with Secondary Education and Teacher Training*. Washington, D.C.: World Bank, pp. 117-22.

Programs for distance training of teachers in Kenya go back some twenty years. The first post-independence Kenya Education Commission, under the chairmanship of Professor Simeon Ominde, was set-up to look into the whole of Kenya's educational system, and has influenced and guided national policy for education since independence. It was the Ominde Commission that first proposed the establishment of radio/correspondence education by the Ministry of Education. The commission urged consideration of a combination of lessons by radio with an approved correspondence course (Government of Kenya, 1964). Thus, the Correspondence Course Unit was set-up in 1967 at the

University College Nairobi (now the University of Nairobi), with initial financial assistance from the United States Agency for International Development.

Since that time, considerable development has taken place and the whole concept and practice of correspondence education in Kenya has expanded to include tutoring at a distance, which is linked to other forms of supportive and integral media. Hence the use of a more comprehensive term—distance education—and the renaming of the Correspondence Course Unit to the Department of Distance Studies, which is part of the College of Education and External Studies of the University of Nairobi.

In-Service Courses for Primary Teachers

The Ministry of Education first launched in-service courses for untrained primary teachers through distance teaching in 1969. The programme continued until 1977, was suspended, and was then revived in 1982. To date, approximately 20,000 primary teachers have received in-service training under this programme, which is likely to continue for some time to come if all the untrained teachers, who account for about 30 per cent of the total force of about 143,000 primary teachers, are to be professionally trained (Table 1).

Table 1 shows that the total number of untrained teachers has continued to rise in the face of increases in the number of schools and pupils. In other words, the proportion of untrained teachers has remained constant at around 30 per cent of the total teaching force. With the introduction of the eight-four-four system (eight years of primary education, four years of secondary, and four years of tertiary) of education in 1985 when the duration of primary education was extended from seven to eight years, an additional 13,500 untrained teachers were recruited into the service with the intention that they would undergo in-service training through distance education.

Organization of Distance Education Programs

The in-service courses are organized on a three-year cycle, that is, each cohort of about 3,000 teachers is enrolled in the distance education programme and takes three years to complete the course before another group is admitted. The learners are required to take a total of fourteen subjects in specified clusters

TABLE 1

Primary Education: Growth of Schools, Pupils, and Teachers, Selected Years

Year	*Number of schools*	*Number of pupils*	*Number of trained teachers*	*Number of untrained teachers*	*Total number of teachers*	*Percentage of trained teachers*
1963	6,058	891.553	17,682	5,045	22,727	77.8
1968	6.135	1,209.680	27,485	10,438	37,923	72.5
1973	6,932	1,816.017	43,990	12,553	56,543	77.8
1978	9,243	2,994.892	63,912	28,134	92,046	69.4
1983	11,856	4,323.921	84,036	35,673	119,709	70.2
1988	13,403	4,986.121	100,319	42,789	143,108	70.1

Source: Ministry of Education.

TABLE 2

Distance Education for Teachers: Required Subjects

First year	*Second year*	*Third year*
Professional studies	Professional studies	Professional studies
English	English	Business education
Mathematics	Mathematics	Home science
Science	Science	Social education and ethics
Riswahili	Kiswahili	Physical education
Music	Arts and crafts	Religious education
	Geography, history, and civics	Geography, history, and civics
	Agriculture	

as shown in Table 2.

The learning media package used in the in-service programme consists of a correspondence component, which comprises about 75 per cent of the course content. This is supported and supplemented by radio lessons broadcast over the Voice of Kenya. In addition, the students participate in face-to-face tuition for a total of seven weeks a year spread over the school holidays at residential primary teachers colleges. The residential component comprises 25 per cent of the course content. Every learner is assessed on a continuous basis throughout the three-year period with grades awarded for performance on the correspondence written assignments, the practical teaching, and the annual examinations.

Correspondence Component

Correspondence study materials constitute the main medium of instruction. They are prepared by the Department of Distance Studies of the University of Nairobi following the teacher education curriculum approved by the Kenya Institute of Education. These study materials are developed in instructional units that are, to a large extent, self-contained and written in a manner that makes them highly interactive. It is assumed that the primary teachers have little or no access to textbooks or reference materials, and the study units therefore include all the basic information needed to understand the subject matter.

To involve the learners in active participation, activities and exercises are built into the text at appropriate intervals. The correspondence course writers adopt, as far as possible, the problem-solving approach in presenting the study materials so as to provide teachers with opportunities to apply what they have learnt.

The actual course content in the in-service programme has two main objectives. First, it helps to update the teachers' academic knowledge of the fourteen subjects taught in primary schools. Second, it helps them acquire the skills and techniques needed to teach the various subjects.

Continuous assessment is an important part of the in-service programme. The teachers are required to submit their written assignments at set intervals for marketing and grading. The task of marking and grading the assignments is carried out by qualified tutors from teachers colleges and secondary schools who are paid on a piecework basis. All these tutors are required to undergo regular training in the methodology of tutoring at a distance. A substantial number of these tutors are recruited from primary teachers colleges to ensure the maintenance of standards prevailing at the pre-service teachers colleges. The Department of Distance Studies is responsible for maintaining all the records of the enrolled teachers and of their performance in the various subjects.

The delivery of study materials and basic textbooks is done through the District Education Offices or, when convenient, during the residential sessions held at the fifteen primary teachers colleges. This helps to minimize the losses and delays experienced when using the postal service.

Radio Component

Radio lessons are designed to support and reinforce the correspondence component. They highlight some of the pertinent points or issues contained in the study units without necessarily repeating or summarizing them. Radio is thus used primarily to motivate the teachers and to pace them as they work through the study materials.

The preparation, scripting, and recording of the radio

programs is done jointly by the Department of Distance Studies and the Educational Media Service of the Kenya Institute of Education. The radio lessons are then broadcast over the Voice of Kenya at regular times with repeat broadcasts throughout the year. Each enrolled teacher receives a broadcast schedule together with any supplementary learning materials.

Over the years it has become evident that most teachers do listen to the radio lessons regularly and have found them useful as supplements to the correspondence study materials. It is also evident from discussions with the teachers and from their written assignments that the radio lessons have had a considerable impact on their learning. They often refer to "what the radio tutor said the other day," or "according to the radio message broadcast last week," and so on.

The radio tutor seems to carry considerable authority, and the apparent immediacy of the messages conveyed through the radio is one of the main benefits listeners often quote. The listeners from the more remote parts of the country depend largely on radio for information about arrangements for residential sessions, examinations dates, and any unforeseen delays in the dispatch of study materials.

An audience survey conducted by the Voice of Kenya in 1985 revealed that some 750,000 people throughout the country had their radios on at the times when the teachers' programs were being broadcast. The "eavesdroppers" included other teachers who were not enrolled, but who found the radio lessons worth listening to.

It has also been established that some of the enrolled teachers have made arrangements to record the radio lessons and have shared them with their colleagues in group learning situations. One conclusion drawn from this modified use of radio programs is that the teachers value the audio component of the learning package, but the inflexibility of the radio schedules was a disadvantage to some of the teachers. The use of audio cassettes introduced the flexibility they needed.

Face-to-Face Component

The face-to-face meetings take four different formats. First are the direct teaching sessions in a classroom situation. The teachers receive instruction on and detailed explanations of some of the difficult concepts they may have encountered in their studies. Second, group discussions are organized to provide an opportunity for the teachers to exchange views and experiences, and to consult with their supervisors and programme administrators. Third, group meetings are held to provide teaching practice under supervision, and to conduct assessment in practical teaching as part of the final evaluation of the teachers. Fourth, written examinations are conducted at designated centers around the country, usually in teachers colleges or secondary schools.

All the residential sessions are held during the school holidays and involve a wide range of professional people. These include representatives from the Ministry's Inspectorate and the In-Service Course Unit, the Kenya Institute of Education, the Department of Distance Studies, the District and Divisional Education Offices, and the Kenya National Examinations Council.

From the institutional standpoint, the face-to-face component of the programme has proved to be the most difficult to organize and execute, and certainly the most demanding in terms of staff time than the correspondence or radio components. It is also the one component that has invariably suffered from budget cuts, and the consequent understaffing and curtailed support services. It has also drawn the largest number of criticisms from the enrolled teachers. Apparently policy-makers have yet to be convinced that distance education, despite its name, does require systematic support services if the learners are to reap the maximum benefit.

Some Lessons Learnt

During its existence, the Kenyan programme of teacher training through distance education has learnt a number of lessons that can be summarized in the following eight points.

1. Teacher Effectiveness

An effective teacher training programme should include a fair amount of teaching of the subject matter that the teacher is supposed to teach, as well as an appropriate repertoire of pedagogical skills in the particular subject. The ideal balance between the academic and the pedagogical content has been a matter of persistent discussion and contention, but the general consensus is that both are important ingredients for teacher effectiveness.

2. Motivation

Although the teachers in the Kenyan programme are generally highly motivated by the monetary benefits that follow their enhanced qualifications and status, their motivation needs to be sustained. In this respect strengthened supervision and professional support should be extended in the teachers to sustain their motivation and increase their professional commitment

3. Cost-effectiveness

Distance education methods are not necessarily cheaper than conventional methods of teacher training, but for the specific needs of unqualified or underqualified teachers, particularly those in rural areas, distance education is the most cost-effective method available. It may also have other broad social and economic benefits for the country or region, for example, retaining dedicated but underqualified teachers in the profession or supporting qualified teachers by giving them extra work as tutors. One thing, however, is clear: the opportunity cost of distance education is significantly lower than for the more conventional teacher training programs.

4. Economies of Scale

Economies of scale can be realized in distance education if the numbers are sufficiently large for one particular programme, or if several programs can share administration, production, delivery, and regional support services. In Kenya, for example, the experiences gained in the use of distance education methods for training primary teachers have been used to train adult literacy teachers (at certificate level) and secondary teachers (at degree level).

5. Cooperation

Close consultation and cooperation among the various departments, organizations, and institutions involved in teacher education programs and clear definition of each entity's responsibilities are very important. However, this takes a great deal of time and effort, and often results in long delays in reaching final decisions. For example, in Kenya the issue regarding teachers certification and awards took more than two years to resolve. The final decision was that the Kenya Institute of Education would develop and review the teacher training curriculum, the Department of Distance Studies would conduct the distance teaching component, the Educational Media Service would prepare the radio programs, the Voice of Kenya would broadcast them, the Ministry's Inspectorate and Field Staff would supervise teaching practice, the Kenya National Examinations Council would conduct the final examinations and award certificates, while the Teachers' Service Commission would recognize the certificates for purposes of employment and promotion.

6. *Training the Distance Educators*

Distance education requires teams of people performing different tasks and working at different levels to accomplish a common institutional goal. They all require orientation and training to equip them with the knowledge, skills, attitudes and approaches that are appropriate to distance education.

7. *Resources*

The central distance education institution must be adequately provided with the necessary physical, fiscal, and human resources to enable it operate efficiently.

8. *Political Support*

The whole programme must have strong political support and commitment.

Looking Ahead

As developing countries continue to grapple with the problems of quantitative expansion of education for all people, the qualitative improvement of education at all levels, and the contingent issue of the cost of education, they must seriously consider alternative delivery systems. In this quest, distance education should play new and expanded roles. A distance education system that may have started as a stop-gap measure and then developed as an alternative system may become an integral part of the mainstream education delivery system. It may just be a matter of time.

Reference

Government of Kenya, 1964, *The Report of the Kenya Education Commission*, Nairobi: Government Printer.

APPENDIX II

Pre-Service Teacher Education at a Distance: The Case of Zimbabwe

B.R.S. Chivore

Context

As in many countries, Zambia faced a demand for teachers that far outstripped the supply from conventional colleges. This example of a pre-service teacher education programme may be useful to educators in other countries. Please note that the full text of this book is available to those with adequate computer capacity at the following. URL:http"//imagebankz.worldbank.org/

Source

Chivore, B.R.S., 1992. "Pre-service Teacher Education at a Distance: The Case of Zimbabwe." In Paud Murphy and Abdelwahed Zhiri, eds. *Distance Education in Anglophone Africa: Experience with Secondary Education and Teacher Training,* Washington, D.C.: World Bank, pp. 103-15.

On attaining independence, virtually all the African countries, embarked on a massive expansion of educational provision at all levels. Zimbabwe is no exception. On attaining independence in 1980, Zimbabwe faced the political, economic, and social challenges that normally accompany attempts to build a new nation. In the social area, the government undertook massive and unprecedented expansion of education at both the primary and secondary levels. In 1979, Zimbabwe had 2,401 primary schools with an enrolment of 819,586 pupils. By 1989, the country had 4,504 primary schools with an enrolment of 2,274,178 pupils. At the secondary level, in 1979 there were 177 secondary schools with an enrolment of 66,215 pupils. By 1989, the country had 1,502 secondary schools with an enrolment of 695,882 pupils. As Table 1 shows, the number of both trained and untrained teachers at the primary level has increased dramatically since independence.

TABLE 1

Teacher Numbers at the Primary Level, 1980-85

Year	*Number of trained teachers*	*Number of untrained teachers*	*Total*
1981	22,654	15,119	37,773
1982	23,699	21,768	45,465
1983	25,954	26,548	52,502
1984	30,424	24,000	54,424
1985	31,496	26,752	58,248

Source: Ministry of Education data.

The demand for teachers outstripped the supply from the country's conventional colleges (Table 2). In response, the government launched a number of unconventional approaches for training non-graduate teachers for both primary and secondary schools.

TABLE 2

Output of Teachers from Conventional Colleges, 1980-83 (Number of Teachers)

Year	*Conventional college output*
1980	680
1981	666
1982	642
1983	1,244

Source: Ministry of Education data.

Teacher Education

Although teacher education is sometimes used interchangeably with teacher training, teacher education is far more than teacher training. Teacher education includes teaching students not only to teach within the four walls of the classroom, but how to base this teaching on sound theoretical knowledge. This knowledge enables teachers to guide their pupils' learning experiences, contribute to the growth and development of people who come into contact with them, and contribute to the development of society at large. Teacher education, whether formal or non-formal, consists of programmed activities and experiences developed by an institution responsible for preparing people to work as professional teachers.

As already mentioned, the government devised new strategies to train teachers to meet the excess demand created by the expansion of educational provision. These include the following:

- The Zimbabwe Integrated National Teacher Education Course (ZINTEC),
- The four-year conventional teacher education programme, and
- The three-year conventional teacher education programme.

The ZINTEC Programme

ZINTEC, initiated in 1981, is the most highly acclaimed post-independence teacher education programme in Zimbabwe. ZINTEC students undertake two long periods of study in one of five colleges at the beginning and end of the programme, and shorter periods each year in between. When the students are not in college they are assigned to schools to teach. During this period they are helped with distance teaching materials and supervised by college lecturers. They are also supervised by school principals and education officers.

The ZINTEC programme was originally based on several assumptions, including:

- Zimbabwe's conventional teacher education system could not meet the new level of demand for teachers.
- New teachers should be produced in line with the enunciated ideology of socialism. As the deputy minister of education (*Herald Newspaper,* April 21, 1982) put it:

"We are instituting an education ideology which should be a means of transforming our society, one that will eventually dispel ignorance, fear, poverty, disease and the mental colonization under which our people have lived for nearly a century."

- The teacher and teacher education have roles to play in Zimbabwe's development process. To that end, on the job training was needed to blend theory with practice.
- Education is a basic human right. Thus, every child in Zimbabwe has a right to education. This meant that the country needed a large teaching force capable of working under difficult and trying conditions.

Rationale for ZINTEC

The decision to start the ZINTEC programme and those that followed it (the three- and four-year programs) was related to the political decision to make primary education free and compulsory. The expansion of primary education meant that more professionally trained teachers were needed. The country could not use the old three-year conventional system to produce teachers because this system produced inadequate number of teachers. Hence ZINTEC student teachers were deployed in primary schools after their initial sixteen-week (now twenty-four-week) orientation courses and received the bulk of their training on the job through distance education.

A second justification for introducing the ZINTEC programme was professional. As stated in the *Handbook on Student Teaching:*

> More and more, in the teaching profession as well as industry, on-the-job training, with increased opportunities for the trainee to integrate the theoretical and practical learning is being seen as having long-term pay-offs both for the individual trainee as well as for the profession. The argument seems to be that it is more effective to train teachers while they are at school for longer periods than was the case under the three-year conventional training (1983, p. 2).

As Ncube (1983, p. 43) put it:

> There is a great deal of interaction during this stage between the student teacher on the one hand and the education world on the other. They (student teachers) see the problems of teaching and education as they are. Whatever solutions emerge are practical in the sense that the student teachers are constantly grappling with those problems both within and outside the school just as they would as full teacher practitioners in a normal school/community.

A third reason put forward to support the ZINTEC programme relates to the cost of training teachers. The programme enabled more teachers to be trained than the three-year conventional scheme without building new colleges. An evaluation (Ministry of Education, 1986) concluded that the cost of training teachers under the ZINTEC programme was cheaper than the three-year conventional programme.

Objectives of the ZINTEC Programme

The main aims and objectives of the ZINTEC programme included the following (Chivore and Masango, 1982, p. 29):

- To address the shortage of primary school teachers through in-service teacher education;
- To develop a teacher education system relevant to the specific problems facing people in their everyday life;
- To develop a teacher education programme guided by Zimbabwe's socialist ideology;
- To effect developmental changes through teacher education;
- To develop a professional teacher with the skills needed to provide pupils with active learning experiences, for example, the concept of education with production; and
- To develop an all round primary teacher with positive attitudes and values who would promote meaningful involvement in community development.

Entry Requirements

To train as a teacher under the ZINTEC programme, the entry

requirements were exactly the same as those needed by any non-university graduate under the conventional programs: five o-levels plus a language (now English language). Each ZINTEC college had three intakes of students per year averaging a total of roughly 800 students per intake. Thus, each year the four ZINTEC colleges enrolled a total of at least 2,400 students.

ZINTEC's Organization

When the ZINTEC programme started, it consisted of the National Center based in Harare and the colleges and their external wings. The National Center consisted of the Administration Unit, the Production Unit, and the Evaluation and Coordination Unit.

The Administration Unit consisted of the director, the senior executive officer, and an executive officer. The Administrative Unit had overall responsibility for the whole programme, including liaising with the Head Office on matters relating to teacher education; liaising with regional officers on the recruitment and deployment of student teachers; liaising with the University of Zimbabwe on certification of students; initiating seminars, workshops, and vacation courses, and generally supervising ZINTEC colleges. It is this unit that was responsible for ensuring that distance education materials were distributed to students through the ZINTEC colleges.

The Evaluation and Coordination Unit was responsible for planning research and evaluating the ZINTEC programme. These duties included assessing the program's aims and objectives, testing distance education modules produced by the Production Unit, coordinating assessment procedures, and assessing human and material resources. At the end of 1982 this unit was moved to the Head Office of the Ministry of Education, where it became part of the Planning Division to evaluate not only ZINTEC, but all the ministry's educational programmes.

The Production Unit was responsible for writing all the distance learning materials student teachers used when they were deployed in the schools, seeing to it that they were dispatched to the regions through ZINTEC colleges, writing and modifying syllabuses, attending seminars in the regions, and testing the written materials. Currently (1990), the Production Unit writes distance teacher education modules for all non-graduate teachers' colleges.

Writing on the role of the National Center, Ncube (1983, p. 46) noted:

> It may be appreciated that the National Center is basically the initiator and coordinator of all ZINTEC activities in Zimbabwe. It is the watchdog of ZINTEC objectives as envisaged by the founders of this teacher education programme. There is also a sense in which the National Center is representative of the new thrust in terms of educational practice and interpretation in Zimbabwe (1983, p. 46).

When the programme started, it had five regional centers: Mashonaland (in Harare), Manicaland (in Mutare), Gwanda (in Gwanda), Masvingo (in Masvingo), and Midlands (in Gweru). Regional centers were responsible for supervising and monitoring students on teaching practice and in their distance education modules. Following a 1982 evaluation (Chivore and Masango, 1982), the regional centers merged with ZINTEC colleges to become the external wings of the colleges.

The four colleges under the programme are Morgan (in Harare), Andrew Louw (in Masvingo), Marymount (in Mutare), and Gwanda (in Gwanda). Their main functions can be divided into two main categories: those relating to the residential courses and those relating to the supervision of students deployed in schools. In 1988, however, only two colleges, Morgan and Gwanda, remained as ZINTEC colleges, but as already noted, as far as distance teacher education is concerned, all non-graduate teachers' colleges receive material from the National Distance Education Center.

As concerns the residential portions of the ZINTEC programme, the colleges are responsible for the initial sixteen-week (now two terms) courses and the final two-term courses. During the initial residential courses, students are introduced to the theory of education, that is psychology, philosophy, and sociology the history of education in Zimbabwe; and applied education. In the subjects taught in primary schools, the final residential courses are devoted to preparing and writing final examinations.

Student Supervision Programme

Students learn both practical teaching and the theory of education. For non-graduate secondary student teachers, the course also includes teaching subjects such as history, geography, mathematics, and science. For non-graduate primary student teachers, distance education also covers applied education subjects, including social studies, English language, and Shona. In summary, the students' major activities include the following:

- Laying the professional foundations (theory of education) through distance education using modules prepared by the Production Unit of the National Distance Education Center;
- Reinforcing the distance education through vacation courses and weekend seminars; and
- Practicing teaching on a full-time basis with the same responsibilities as qualified teachers.

During teaching practice, lecturers visit students at least once each term. School principals, district education officers, and education officers also supervise the student teachers while they are on teaching practice. These officials submit reports on each student at least once a term to the students' colleges.

Certification

Like all non-graduate teachers, candidates who train under the ZINTEC programme are certified by the University of Zimbabwe, which maintains standards across the country. The university's Department of Teacher Education is responsible for assessing, approving, and monitoring the syllabuses followed by ZINTEC colleges. It brings in external examiners to moderate examinations (and even sends syllabuses to external examiners for moderation).

During their first two residential terms, students are assessed through assignments and short written tests, which help determine whether or not they proceed to the second phase. Note that examinations and tests taken during the students' first year are not used as part of their final assessment.

When the students are deployed in schools, in addition to teaching practice, they write assignments marked by their college tutors. A student is supposed to be visited at least five times by college lecturers or education officers before certification.

Since the programme started, pass rates have been relatively high and the dropout rate insignificant. Table 3 shows the pass rates for seven recent programme intakes.

TABLE 3

ZINTEC Programme Pass Rates at the University of Zimbabwe, Intakes 1-7

Intake	*Total enrolment*	*Number of students graduating*	*Percentage graduating*
1	729	540	70.1
2	687	498	72.5
3	111	636	81.9
4	806	672	83.4
5	795	647	81.4
6	778	687	88.3
7	722	653	90.4
Total	5,294	4,333	82.0

Source: University of Zimbabwe, Department of Teacher Education.

The percentage of those who finally qualified is higher than the figures provided. This is because the total percentages above exclude those candidates who did not complete the course with the rest of their intake. In 1989, for example, Morgan ZINTEC College held a special graduation ceremony for deferred students. The actual percentage for those who completed their course could be between 86 and 97 per cent. It is interesting to note that the percentage of those who passed improved from 70.1 per cent in intake 1 to 90.4 per cent in intake 7. The average number of students who passed was 82.0 per cent. The other important point is that there is no significant difference between ZINTEC and conventionally trained primary teachers in terms of achievement as measured by performance in examinations and overall pass rates.

Distance Education in Conventional Teachers' Colleges

Following experiences gained in the ZINTEC programme, the mode of training non-graduate primary and secondary teachers changed from three to four years. As a national report (1984, p. 17) observed:

> The success of ZINTEC revealed by the evaluation exercise resulted in the "Zintecisation" of teacher training colleges. In place of the 3 years conventional training programme, a four year course comprising first year residential, second year on-the-job, third year residential and fourth year on-the-job has been instituted.

However, as already noted; in 1988 the training of non-graduate teachers in conventional colleges reverted to three years. Student teachers spent their first and third years at college and their second year in the schools as full-time teachers receiving their tuition through distance education modules from the National Center for Distance Education.

Evaluation

Since the ZINTEC programme started, the Ministry of Education, the United Nations Children's Fund (UNICEF), and other interested parties have carried out several evaluations. Whenever the ZINTEC programme was evaluated, conventional teacher education programs were also evaluated.

Reasons for Evaluating the ZINTEC Programme

ZINTEC underwent major evaluations in 1982 and 1986. The following were some of the main reasons why the ZINTEC programme was evaluated (Chivore and Masango, 1982):

- To determine the degree to which ZINTEC was attaining its purposes, aims, and objectives;
- To provide evidence on the value of the ZINTEC programme necessary to those, both internal and external, providing funding;
- To provide data on the programme and on teacher education needed for general educational planning (covering, for example, teacher supply and demand, college staffing, admission procedures, and the dual system of teacher education);
- To collect data essential for the continued ongoing improvement of the programme;

- To have a critical but objective analysis of the main problems encountered and recommendations on how to handle them, beneficial not only to ZINTEC, but to education in general and teacher education in particular;
- To determine the impact and effectiveness of ZINTEC student supervision; and
- To assess the cost-effectiveness of this type of teacher education.

Highlights of the Evaluation Findings

Only those findings with a bearing on distance education are discussed. These include ZINTEC's organization, staffing, student supervision, and the effectiveness of distance education.

ZINTEC Organization

As already noted, following the 1982 evaluation, the Evaluation and Coordination Unit was moved to the Planning Division of the Ministry of Education. Chivore and Masango (1982, p. 37), the report's authors, recommended that "the Evaluation Unit should become part of the Head Office, Planning Division but should continue monitoring such projects as the ZINTEC programme as well as other innovations that may be launched."

When the ZINTEC programme started, its regional centers and colleges were separate entities. The 1982 evaluation recommended that the colleges and regional centers should be administratively and physically united to facilitate closer coordination and cooperation between field- and college-based lecturers, and efficient use of facilities such as distance education modules and libraries.

Staffing

The average lecturer-student ratio at the colleges was 1:40 in 1982, while the field lecturer-student ratio was 1:60. This staff shortage had adverse implications for the lecturers, whose workloads became very heavy in terms of visiting students, marking distance education assignments, supervising both theoretical and practical work, and holding vacation seminars. The staff shortage was not confined to ZINTEC colleges, but was also apparent in conventional colleges, which by 1982 had introduced distance education as part of their mode of training.

The quality and relevance of education in a developing country such as Zimbabwe depends on the quality and relevance of the teacher. Both evaluations established that the vast majority of ZINTEC lecturers, as well as those in conventional colleges, were university graduates, some with higher degrees, trained to teach at the secondary level. Those lecturers teaching at the primary level were not trained to teach at that level. Those teaching at secondary teachers' colleges were not trained in teacher education, let alone distance teacher education. Hence the evaluations recommended refresher courses in the form of workshops. Some candidates were sent abroad to take short courses in distance education.

Student Supervision

Field supervision of student teachers by lecturers formed one of the most important activities in the training of teachers through distance education. The 1982 evaluation in particular indicated that 80 per cent of the student teachers were visited once per term, 8 per cent were visited twice, while 12 per cent had not been visited at the time of the evaluation. This is an inadequate number of visits, but was representative of what was taking place in the programme as a whole at the time.

Submissions made to the Evaluations and Coordination Unit by a field lecturer voiced concern about the inadequacy of visits. One college wrote: "It is impossible to visit students regularly because of tutor-student ratios." Another college requested "more staff to facilitate for more visits to students and more face-to-face interventions with students." At the same time, 96 per cent of the students who took part in the 1982 evaluation stated that field supervision by field lecturers was inadequate. The student teachers rated this as the most crucial problem. The 1986 evaluation also highlighted the inadequacy of field supervision.

The 1986 evaluation analyzed the quality of the supervision carried out. It reported that lecturers spent more time checking schemes of work, lesson plans, and records rather than helping students reinforce concepts and skills and link theory with practice. This was partly due to the lack of funds, vehicles, and staff.

Effectiveness of Distance Education

The Evaluation Unit pre-tested modules produced by the Production Unit to assess their content, relevance, and comprehensiveness. One simple method used to determine if students understood the modules was to ask them to underline words and concepts in the modules that they did not understand. Students were also asked to define or explain certain terms such as hypothesis or telegraphic utterances. As the 1982 (p. 103) report notes: "In their written assignments, the majority of students failed to explain terms using their own words." Thus, it became clear that some of the modules were beyond the students' comprehension. Thus, the report recommended that the Production Unit produce simpler modules that reflected the student teachers' academic level.

As part of their continuous assessment, both ZINTEC and conventional students write assignments and projects as directed in their modules. The evaluations established that there were problems in the marking of these assignments. Lecturers were not up-to-date with the marking and were slow to return students' distance education assignments. This developed into a vicious cycle as students became demotivated and started to submit their assignments late. The end-result was that students wrote and submitted assignments without the necessary feedback vital for their professional and academic growth. As the 1986 (p. 6) report observed: "The delay meant that students did not benefit from the tutors' comments since they (students) wrote the next assignment before receiving the first, second and sometimes third assignment." Other reasons why student teachers were late in submitting their assignments were a lack of reference materials at their schools of deployment, inability to carry out research, heavy work load (since they were also full-time teachers), and poor postal services in some areas.

Effectiveness of ZINTEC-Trained Teachers

Teachers' effectiveness can be rated on their skills at lesson planning, using teaching and learning aids, classroom management, class management, language and communication, education with production, education and the community, extramural activities, pupil evaluation, and record-keeping. The 1982 evaluation found that the majority of student teachers were effective at extramural activities, language and communication, teaching and learning aids, class management, record-keeping, and classroom management. They were relatively ineffective at lesson planning, class evaluation, education with production, and education and the community. The reasons for this relative ineffectiveness included confusion between aims and objectives; some principals who told student teachers to follow the lesson and planning formats of their schools, with the result that student teachers could not put into practice what they were taught at college; and some colleges that did not equip their students with proper planning guidelines. In the 1986 evaluation, however, and in other subsequent studies (Chivore, 1985, 1986a, 1989b) planning was not among the weaknesses of the ZINTEC students.

The Effectiveness of Distance-Trained Teachers Once Qualified

The 1982 and 1986 evaluations of teacher effectiveness were carried out among student teachers. It is common knowledge that the fine efforts made when candidates are student teachers often evaporate once these same candidates become qualified teachers. Hence the importance of evaluating the effectiveness of professionally trained teachers (though admittedly distance education alone was not the only approach used to train these teachers).

Chivore (1989a), along with fourteen experienced educators, carried out a pilot study on the effectiveness of teachers trained since independence in the Harare region. The study analyzed teacher effectiveness in several areas, including class management. This included lesson introduction, lesson development, teacher-pupil interaction, questioning techniques, class control, pupil participation, and the amount of written work given. In five of the seven items—lesson introduction, teacher-pupil interaction, questioning techniques, class control, and amount of work given—ZINTEC-trained teachers were rated as the most effective. The pilot study observed that:

> In order of strength, as far as class management was concerned, based on the type of training received, the posit on was as follows: ZINTEC, four-year conventional and finally three-year conventional (Chivore, 1989a, p. 20).

Even though this pilot study focused only on the Harare region, it is heartening to note that in terms of effectiveness, training on the job using distance education seems to be an effective method of training pre-service, non-graduate teachers.

Problems Encountered by Student Teachers Trained Through Distance Education

During both the 1982 and 1986 evaluations, student teachers were asked to write down problems they encountered during their training, particularly during the deployment period. The problems mentioned by these students were basically similar to those already discussed. They included the following:

- Inadequate supervision by the lecturers;
- Lack of feedback on assignments and projects to students from lecturers;
- Lack of books during deployment;
- Poor postal services in some areas that hindered communication between colleges and students; and
- Relatively heavy teaching loads, which resulted in some student teachers failing to strike a proper balance between their duties as student teachers and their duties as full-time teachers.

Other studies have confirmed most of the above problems (Chivore, 1986a, 1986b). The government has attempted to minimize most of these problems by implementing recommendations made in the evaluations.

The Impact of Training Teachers through Distance Education

It is not possible here to cover all the contributions distance education has made in training non-graduate teachers in Zimbabwe. Despite the problems noted above, the ZINTEC programme has had tremendous achievements, including implications for the cost-effectiveness of teacher training and in improved output of trained teachers. The result is that distance education has become a permanent feature of Zimbabwe's system of teacher education.

The 1986 ZINTEC evaluation concluded:

> From the information collected by the evaluation team, it was established that the ZINTEC programme was cost-effective. It was found to be more cost-effective than what used to be the conventional Teacher Education programme. Furthermore the ZINTEC programme produced more teachers than the conventional programme.

Between 1980 and 1988, a total of 17,455 primary teachers completed their training in Zimbabwe (Table 4).

TABLE 4

Number of Primary Teachers Trained, 1980-88

Year	*Number of associate colleges*	*Number of teachers certified*
1980	5	322
1981	7	618
1982	9	809
1983	9	1,379
1984	13	1,958
1985	14	2,384
1986	14	2,162
1987	14	4,429
1988	14	4,394
Total	17,455	

Source: University of Zimbabwe, Department of Teacher Education.

Note that the figure of 17,455 trained teachers includes only those candidates who completed their training at colleges that received associate status from the University of Zimbabwe. The figure excludes referred and deferred candidates, most of whom completed their training. Consequently, the final figure should be higher.

Note also the increase in the number of trained teachers from 1983 on. This is due to the teacher output from ZINTEC colleges.

Teacher Education in Southern Africa

Almost every country in southern Africa emphasizes the

need for universal primary education. However, one of the impediments that militates against universal primary education is the lack of trained teachers. Another problem seems to be too much experimentation in the training of teachers. During the past ten years, Zimbabwe has had three types of pre-service teacher training. These different patterns meant that the country has not developed a single system of teacher education based on well thought out plans and evaluations. Worse still, the ZINTEC programme, which according to pilot studies (Chivore, 1989a) is producing competent teachers, is apparently being systematically phased out even though the shortage of professionally trained teachers persists. Distance education is one way to solve the problem of too few trained teachers in southern Africa, especially for newly independent countries such as Namiba.[*sic*]

Conclusion

Since attaining its independence, Zimbabwe has invested heavily in education. In the process of that investment, the government has introduced various types of teacher education programs. Prominent among them was the ZINTEC programme, which brought with it distance education as a mode of training pre-service, non-graduate teachers. This innovation affected all forms of pre-service, non-graduate teacher education, in that for the first time in the country's history distance education played a prominent role in teacher education. What is now urgently required is a systematic and thorough impact evaluation of teachers trained since independence to assess their effectiveness. This is crucial because if money is spent producing incompetent, inefficient, and ineffective educators it is money wasted.

REFERENCES

Chivore, B.R.S., 1985, "Recruitment and Training of Non-Graduate Secondary Teachers in Zimbabwe Since Independence," Ph.D. thesis, University of London, Institute of Education. Unpublished.

Chivore, B.R.S., 1986a, "Teacher Education in Post-Independent Zimbabwe: Problems and Possible Solutions," *Journal of Education for Teaching*, 12:3.

Chivore, B.R.S., 1986b, "Teacher Education in Zimbabwe: New Strategies, Problems, and Possible Solutions. In B.W. Treffgarne, ed., *Education in Zimbabwe*, Occasional Papers, 9, London: University of London, Institute of Education, Department of International and Comparative Education.

Chivore, B.R.S., 1989a, *An Evaluation of the Effectiveness of Primary Teachers Trained Since Zimbabwe Attained Independence.* Unpublished.

Chivore, B.R.S., 1989b, "Zimbabwe's Experiences in the Evaluation of Distance Education Programmes," In M. Simonson and S. Zvacek, eds., *Proceedings of Distance Education,* Seminar papers, Iowa: University of Iowa.

Chivore, B.R.S., and R.B. Masango, 1982, *An Interim Assessment Report on the Effectiveness of the ZINTEC Programme and Implications for Teacher Education in Zimbabwe,* Harare, Zimbabwe: Ministry of Education and Culture, ZINTEC National Centre.

Ministry of Education, Planning Division, 1986, *An Evaluation of the Impact of the ZINTEC Programme—A Summary Report,* Harare, Zimbabwe.

Ncube, A.M., 1983, "The Zimbabwe Integrated National Teacher Education Course (ZINTEC)." In U. Buds and J. Greenland, eds., *In-Service Education and Training of Primary School Teachers in Anglophone Africa,* Baden Baden, Switzerland: Nomos Verlagergeseschaft.

APPENDIX III

Distance Education for Teacher Education: Hong Kong Experience

Ronnie Carr, Yvonne Fung and Shui Kin Chan

Open University of Hong Kong, Koivloon, Hong Kong

The Open University of Hong Kong (OUHK) is one of an increasing number of institutions offering teacher education programmes through distance education. This article focuses largely on one of the programmes from the OUHK's School of Education and Languages—the in-service Bachelor of Education (Honours) in Primary Education (BEDHPE). Some examples of teacher education programmes at a distance are discussed, followed by a brief review of the nature of in-service teacher education and the features of high-quality distance education materials and learner support systems. The article then presents the results of an evaluation of the above programme. On the basis of survey findings, it is argued that distance education programmes that are well designed and efficiently implemented can provide an effective, flexible alternative to the traditional approach to in-service teacher education.

Introduction

Until relatively recently, teacher education programmes in Hong Kong for primary school teachers were exclusively at the Certificate level and provided by the Colleges of Education, which in 1994 were amalgamated to become the Hong Kong Institute of Education. In 1982, an overseas Visiting Panel, invited by the Hong Kong Government to undertake an overall review of the education system commented that the lack of prestige of primary school teaching was 'aggravated by the fact that there are no degree courses to prepare primary school teachers' (Llewellyn *et al*, 1982, p. 90). In 1988, one local university started to offer this degree on a part-time basis for serving primary teachers. However, fewer than 50 places were provided each year and the programme focused on leadership and educational management for principals.

In 1992, the Education Commission [1] recognised that Hong Kong teachers were facing an ever-increasing range of challenges in areas such as pupils' behavioural and emotional problems, curriculum innovation and school management reform. It proposed the development of in-service degree programmes for primary teachers, making use of 'distance learning combined with substantial face-to-face tuition'. It further suggested that the then Open Learning Institute of Hong Kong (OLI),[2] which was set-up to offer self-funding distance learning degree courses for adults, could be a provider.

With an area of less than 1100 km^2, distance and geographical barriers do not present a significant problem in Hong Kong, and it may be difficult to imagine why a distance learning institution is needed. However, 'distance' is not simply a geographical concept; the high levels of commitment to family and work that characterise Hong Kong's population also constitute powerful barriers to adult participation in programmes which require frequent attendance at lectures/tutorials. As the Education Commission (1992) recognised, a flexible and cost-effective mode of learning was necessary for the upgrading of serving teachers. With a traditional face-to-face approach, it would have been very difficult to meet its initial target of having 35% graduate posts (for roughly 6000 teachers) in primary schools by 2007[3] and would have required very substantial public funding.

The Open University of Hong Kong (OUHK)—at that time, the Open Learning Institute (OLI)—responded to the Education Commission's report by acting as the leader of a consortium in developing a Bachelor of Education (Honours) in Primary Education (BEDHPE) through distance learning, the first course being presented in April 1994.

Initial Reactions to the Programme

The Hong Kong government's decision to utilise distance education for upgrading primary school teachers to degree level provoked considerable scepticism—and even some overt criticism. For example, several local educators expressed the view in the press that the government's thinking had been dominated by cost considerations and that quality would suffer in such large-scale (by Hong Kong standards) programmes, which would inevitably be second-class in comparison with the 'normal' approach.

Such reactions can be attributed in part at least to a variety of factors in the educational and cultural context of Hong Kong:

1. At a general level, particularly since the OLI had been established as recently as 1989, the concept of distance learning was still relatively unfamiliar to many academics in other Hong Kong tertiary institutions and to the community at large. Certainly, few were aware of the extent to which distance education had become an international phenomenon, with the establishment of dedicated distance teaching universities and dual-mode institutions in many parts of the world. Often judgements were based at best on knowledge/experience of overseas offerings presented locally that adopted the label 'distance education', but which by no means always exhibited the features that would be generally considered to be essential in any high-quality distance education system.

   Many people found it difficult to visualise how effective learning can be achieved through using learning materials with only a limited provision of face-to-face contact—especially in a professional area such as teacher education in which extensive face-to-face interaction with students has traditionally been seen as an essential element.
2. The philosophy of providing a 'second chance' for adults as a contribution to lifelong learning and human resource development was not fully appreciated by many educators in higher education and some others in the wider community. As in many other open universities around the world, the OUHK has an open access policy for most of its undergraduate programmes—a concept that was very radical in Hong Kong, which for a long time had an extremely competitive education system in which university education was the preserve of a small elite. For the

programme under consideration, there are, in fact, entry requirements—possession of a Teachers' Certificate and a minimum of 2 years' teaching experience—but all qualified applicants are admitted. The lack of any further selection mechanism for the programme was sometimes viewed as allowing 'less capable' students to pursue a degree, leading ultimately to the production of 'second-rate' graduates. The possibility of combining greater 'openness' in entry with the maintenance of graduate standards at the exit point was not given serious consideration by those who questioned the institution's access policy.

3. Even where there was an acceptance of the potential of its methodology and philosophy in certain contexts, there were perhaps some residual doubts about how well distance education would operate in Hong Kong. There is a widespread perception that the teaching methods here are largely expository and teacher-directed, with 'students displaying almost unquestioning acceptance of the knowledge of the teacher or lecturer . . . [which] may be explained as an extension or transfer of the Confucian ethic of filial piety' (Murphy, 1987). While it may be argued that this is something of an overstatement in the light of student behaviour in at least some Hong Kong classrooms, the continuing influence of the Confucian tradition in what may on the surface appear to be a thoroughly Westernised system should not be underestimated. Would a distance education system with its more student-centred approach operate effectively in such an educational context? Would tensions arise between distance education's greater emphasis on independent learning and the collectivist values in the wider culture?

Despite the raising of such doubts by some of the educational community, the University launched its B.Ed. (Hons.) in April 1994, with an initial enrolment of over 900 students. Registrations have continued at a reasonable level since then, despite the highly competitive environment in which the programme functions. By 2000, there had been four cohorts of graduates (a total of over

1200) and over 1800 students were studying for the degree.

This article provides some illustrative examples of the use of distance education for teacher education in a range of countries. It then outlines briefly the features of effective in-service teacher education, and considers the ways in which the OUHK distance learning materials for the BEDHPE programme attempt to put; these into practice. Finally, it reports the findings of a programme evaluation survey.

Teacher Education in a Distance Mode

A World-wide Development

The OUHK's 'distance' approach to teacher education was not, of course, a novel development. It had already been used extensively to supplement the traditional college-based approach in a wide range of developing countries, particularly in Africa (e.g. Brophy and Dudley, 1981, 1982, 1983; Perraton, 1984; Coldevin and Naidu, 1989)—and in, for example, Australia (Evans and Nation, 1991, 1993) and the United Kingdom (Prescott and Robinson, 1993).

As long ago as the early 1980s, Brophy and Dudley reported that over 60 distance education programmes for teacher education had been established in more than 40 countries for a variety of purposes:

- initial training of teachers about to enter the teaching force, or already teaching;
- upgrading unqualified but experienced teachers; and
- continuing education of those already experienced and qualified.

Perhaps particularly relevant in the context of this article are the teacher education programmes at a range of levels currently offered in large-scale Open Universities, such as the Open University of the United Kingdom, the Open University of Sri Lanka, Allama Iqbal Open University (Pakistan), Sukhothai Thammathirat Open University (Thailand) and Universitas Terbuka (Indonesia).

In general, distance education for teacher education has a number of clear advantages, for example:

- it makes it possible for a few course developers to reach a large number of students, including those in remote areas (helping in the process to counteract the tendency for college-trained teachers to move to urban areas to work);
- the student-teachers do not need to be replaced as they continue to work while they learn; and
- it can achieve considerable economies of scale since, once the system has been established and the teaching materials developed, the cost of enrolling extra students is relatively low.

Of course the picture is not all positive. Distance education programmes have often been characterised by high dropout rates, and the mass-produced materials have not always been of a high quality in terms of content and pedagogy (e.g. Garrison, 1993; Moblda, 1997). Nor is distance education necessarily always cheaper (Rumble, 1997); for example, the size of the student body, the amount of face-to-face tutoring and the sophistication of the media employed all have a particularly important bearing on the actual cost. Finally, there have been very few analyses of the comparative effects of traditional and distance programmes on participants' ability to teach—though the findings of, for instance, Brophy and Dudley (1981, 1983), Mahlck and Temu (1989) and Nielsen and Tatto (1993) suggested that teachers studying through distance programmes can teach as effectively as those involved in traditional programmes.

The Nature of In-service Teacher Education

Qualified serving teachers have already acquired the basic knowledge, understanding and skills of teaching, and may also have derived considerable benefit from their career experience. However, teachers' informal learning, important though it is, may limit their development, so there is still a need for planned programmes in order to accelerate their professional growth. Day (1999) suggested that such growth could be additive or transformative. While additive growth expands teachers' repertoires, it cannot guarantee willingness on their part to initiate change in practice. If programmes are to be genuinely concerned with the promotion of professional development, therefore, they must first attempt to change teachers' beliefs, conceptions and attitudes, and help them to reconstruct their personal theories about teaching.

One way of doing this is to develop teachers' self-awareness and reflection—stimulating them to examine their existing context and practice for improvement and the development of new perspectives. This requires that teacher education programmes are designed from the teachers' perspective. That is, as learners, they must be engaged in recognising and analysing their experiences for new learning—a basis for reflective action—and in this process be helped to transfer their tacit knowledge into 'working' or 'practical' knowledge (the terms used to characterise the nature of teacher knowledge by Yinger and Hendricks-Lee, 1993, and Jarvis, 1997, respectively).

To what extent can such complex processes be mediated through distance education?

Distance Learning Materials for Teacher Education

Clearly, the subject content of self-instructional materials must be accurate, comprehensive and at the right level of academic demand, but in developing them considerable attention needs to be given also to pedagogical aspects.

Well-designed self-instructional materials are very different in structure and style from expository texts, such as lecture notes and journal articles. For example, they typically have a clear statement of aims and objectives, and include a range of other access devices—course guides, advance organisers, self-assessment tests, clear and consistent use of headings; and sub-headings, summaries, glossaries and icons of various kinds, etc. Also, drawing on theories such as Holmberg's 'guided pedagogic conversation' (1989), they are written in a more personal and conversational style.

In learning through such materials, students are not involved in a passive process of uncritical assimilation of information, but are guided to interact with the developers' ideas. The materials—whatever the medium—attempt to provide two-way communication in which 'learners interact with texts to construct their own meanings' (Morgan, 1995) and evaluate their learning, thus promoting a deep learning approach.

The most obvious way in which this is done is through

'activities' built into the text that, for example, attempt to replicate the sorts of questions good tutors would raise in a classroom context, or ask learners to relate their knowledge to their own situation and think critically about their actions (Rowntree, 1992); and, where appropriate, explanatory feedback is provided.

The materials developed by the OUHK for the B.Ed. (Hons.) programme embed such activities into the study units, asking students to, for instance:

- recall a teaching (or learning) experience and evaluate it in the light of knowledge gained from the course; comment on examples of how teachers acted in certain situations and draw comparisons with their own experience;
- evaluate the applicability of theories covered in the study units to local classroom practices; and
- review their philosophy or stance on a range of educational issues; carry out and evaluate practical work in the classroom or school.

Printed materials of this kind—supplemented where necessary by, for example, audio- and video-cassettes or CD-ROMs—help learners to analyse and reflect on their practice, and construct new working knowledge based on theory. The student assignments in the 'classroom teaching subjects' in this B.Ed. programme include the planning, implementation and evaluation of small-scale projects in which the learners play the role of 'teachers as researchers', thus giving them the opportunity to reflect, self-assess and develop professionally.

Learner Support System

Quality distance education systems need to include an element of tutor/counsellor support to provide a 'personal' dimension in what may otherwise be a rather impersonal system. However well produced the self-instructional materials are, students must have someone to turn to when facing difficulties in their studies, for a variety of reasons. For instance, it is unrealistic to expect them all to function as completely independent learners at the outset, particularly if they have been used to being taught in very traditional ways and, of course, with adult learners, not all their problems are purely academic in nature, though they may affect their attainment.

In the OUHK model, learners are allocated to a tutor who not only holds a limited number of tutorial meetings as well as tutoring by telephone, but also assesses and—very important—teaches through assignments in the process attempting to develop a dialogue with the learners. For the B.Ed. programme under review, Tutorial Manuals with suggested activities are provided to both the tutors and the students, and (perhaps more so in Educational Studies than in other subject areas) exchange of experience and a focus on the relationship between theory and practice are emphasised. Also, although this is still at a relatively early stage in this programme, on-line elements are being introduced into the courses to enhance communication between the students and their tutors/course coordinators, and among the students.

Given the importance of the tutor's roles, rigorous selection procedures are essential. Where there are problems in recruiting an adequate number of good tutors—as has sometimes been the case in the B.Ed. programme—thresholds should be set for student registration to maintain quality. Once appointed, staff development and monitoring of tutor performance are also clearly required. In the OUHK's case, tutors attend two initial orientation meetings, followed by at least three further meetings during the academic year, which focus on issues related to course content, tutorial strategies, assignment marking and commenting, and developing students' study skills. Also, the quality of tutors' performance: in grading and teaching is assessed by the course coordinators through, for example, the monitoring of sample assignments and periodic visits to Tutorial Centres.

Evaluation of the Programme

Assessments of the effectiveness of distance education programmes have typically focused on variables such as:

- cost-efficiency;
- student numbers;
- completion rates; and
- examination results.

An indication of the student numbers has been given earlier and, in brief, for all courses, both the completion rates (usually ranging from slightly less than 90 to over 95%) and the examination pass rates (usually over 90% and sometimes even 100%) have been very satisfactory.

For teacher education, however, such measures involve a rather narrow concept of effectiveness. Ideally, in such a professional area, programme evaluation should include a direct assessment of the impact of the programme on classroom practice—what Perraton (1993) refers to as the 'Achilles heel' of teacher education, in both distance and traditional systems. In this case, in part because this in-service B.Ed. programme did not include observation visits to schools, a more limited approach was adopted. Students were asked, for example, to report on the usefulness and relevance of what they had learned (as in, for instance, Robinson, 1993) and to assess the extent to which they had attempted to implement what they had gained from the programme in their classrooms (cf. Holmes *et al*, 1993).

Methodology

The evaluation made use of two separate, but similar, questionnaires mailed to all those who had graduated by 1999 (n = 639) and students who had completed 70 out of the 80 credits required for the programme (n = 691). The student sample was selected on the basis that the size was manageable and that the students involved should have completed a substantial portion of the programme. Both questionnaires contained two parts:

> Ten structured items in which respondents were asked to indicate the extent to which they agreed in each case. These items covered three areas, namely, the professional relevance of the programme, the programme's impact on the teachers and the support provided. An open-ended section in which respondents were asked to write down their views on using a distance-learning mode.

In addition, the questionnaire for the graduates also collected some demographic data, such as their posts in schools, their years of graduation, and whether they had been promoted or had changed their posts since graduation.

Results

The views of graduates and students on the programme and the academic support they received are presented in Table I, with the responses from students in brackets.

TABLE I

	% Responses			
	Strongly agree	*Agree*	*Disagree*	*Strongly disagree*
Professional relevance and applicability of the programme:				
It provided students with greater insight into educational issues	17.1 (19.3)	79.1 (78.1)	3.8 (2.6)	0 (0)
What was learned was applicable to work	8.2 (10.0)	82.0 (79.7)	9.2 (10.0)	0.6 (0.3)
The courses were academically demanding	5.8 (7.6)	70.9 (71.1)	23 (21.3)	0.3 (0)
Not much professional knowledge was gained through the programme	1.3 (3.3)	19.6 (17.3)	66.8 (69.4)	12.3 (10.0)
The programme structure met the needs of most primary school teachers	9.8 (9.3)	80.7 (82.4)	9.2 (8.3)	0.3 (0)
The courses were usually very theoretical and did not relate much to practice	1.6 (1.3)	27.7 (25.8)	66.9 (69.6)	3.8 (3.3)
Impact of the programme on the learners:				
It helped students to become independent learners	19.6 (18.3)	74.4 (75.8)	6.0 (6.0)	0 (0)
Students enjoyed studying the programme	7.4 (8.6)	64.5 (64.8)	27.5 (26.3)	0.6 (0.3)
Adequacy of academic support received:				
In general, the course coordinators were supportive	3.3 (2.7)	64.9 (66.2)	29.6 (29.1)	2.3 (2.0)
In general, the tutors helped students to understand the course material better	2.9 (2.3)	74.0 (75.6)	21.8 (20.7)	1.3 (1.3)

Table I: Responses to the questionnaire.

Academic Demands and Applicability to Work

The graduate and student responses were comparable and very positive. The majority of the respondents (over 75%) agreed or strongly agreed that the programme was academically demanding. (The academic quality of the course materials and assessment demands had already been commented or by external assessors and examiners.) Also, though teacher education courses offered by higher education institutions have often been criticised in the past for their lack of relevance to school needs and their inability to make research findings accessible to teachers (Day, 1999), the responses in this case suggested otherwise. The vast majority of the graduates and students (around 90%) considered that the programme met their needs in primary schools and that what they had learned was applicable to their teaching. About 70% in each case disagreed with the view that the courses were 'too theoretical'. Comments from some respondents in the open-ended section of the questionnaire reinforced the findings from the quantitative data, for example:

> *It gives teachers a chance to enhance their professional knowledge and increase their competitiveness.*
>
> *Learning can be applied immediately to work.*
>
> *The course materials use concrete examples to illustrate abstract theories, so that students can understand easily.*

From the learners' viewpoint, then, the balance between the academic and practical elements made the programme valuable for professional development.

Insight into Educational Issues

Almost unanimously (about 97%), the respondents agreed that the programme provided them with greater insight into educational issues. As mentioned earlier, the extending of teachers' skills and knowledge may be superficial if their attitudes and beliefs remain unchanged. By helping teachers to analyse educational issues from multiple perspectives, they are encouraged to evaluate their own values and beliefs, and construct new personal theories—a very important aspect of teacher growth to which the programme appears to have contributed.

Personal Impact on Learners

Two other findings from the survey gave a strong indication that the use of learner-centred materials had met with considerable success. The first was that a very high percentage of both graduates and students (94% in both cases) agreed that pursuing the degree had helped them to become independent learners. This is very significant as degree study involves intensive learning for teachers over only a limited period; and it is essential that they continue to improve and enrich themselves. As in most parts of the world, Hong Kong is entering the information age where lifelong learning becomes fundamentally important for all its citizens and the creation of 'a life-long learning society' has been advocated by the Education Commission (2000) in its recent proposals on educational reform. That teachers become lifelong learners is clearly critical if they are to promote this capacity successfully among their pupils.

The second finding was that a substantial proportion (almost 75%) of respondents agreed that they had enjoyed studying the programme, indicating that it had a positive affective impact on them. Hargreaves (1995) criticised in-service teacher development Initiatives that attend only to rationality and strategy, underplaying the importance of teachers' feeling and emotions. The fact that studying this degree programme was considered an enjoyable experience by most of the learners should help to sustain their interest in learning throughout their careers.

Again, some responses in the open-ended section also illustrated these two findings, for example:

> *Teachers have the ability for self-learning and the distance learning mode can develop this ability further.*
>
> *Distance learning helps to develop self-discipline.*
>
> *The design of the courses is systematic, which is suitable for independent study.*

Academic Support

With respect to the provision of academic support, about 70% of the respondents agreed that the full-time academic staff had been supportive and almost 80% that the part-time tutors had helped them to understand the courses better. However, not all comments in the open-ended section were positive on this aspect. While a few students commented favourably on the support provided through tutorials, workshops and telephone tuition, a somewhat larger number suggested that there should be more face-to-face tutorials, and that the quality of the tutors varied, for example:

> *I prefer to have more tutorials and more interaction between tutors and students.*
>
> *Some tutors cannot help us understand the course content.*
>
> *We would understand the course materials better if tutors can lead us in the tutorials.*

Such views on the extent of face-to-face tutorials and the variability in the quality of tutors merit serious consideration as they touch on a potential conflict between the philosophy and practice of distance education and the dominant beliefs of at least some students. Previous studies (e.g. Chan, 1994; Fung and Carr, 1999, 2000) have shown that OUHK students value highly academic support from their tutors which enhances their understanding of the course materials, but they tend to prefer a traditional lecture-type format for tutorials, especially at the early stage in their studies. Their preference for tutor-centred tutorials reflects the largely transmissive and examination-orientated teaching methods which most of them have experienced in secondary school.

Although such an expressed desire for more face-to-face tutorials, with tutors 'leading' the group, are not representative of the responses in general, they signal the importance of:

> *ensuring high standards of tutoring through appropriate selection of part-time staff and effective staff development;*
>
> *a continuing need to illustrate to students the role of face-to-face tuition within a distance system and, more generally, the value of less teacher<entred modes of tutoring such as discussion (whole- and small-group), student presentations, role play, etc.*

The tendency for students to prefer a fairly directive approach in tutorials might appear to confirm the belief that Hong

Kong students are compliant and passive. In this regard it is worth-noting, however, that Fung and Carr (1999) found that, even when actual practice in tutorials deviated significantly from students' preferred formats, most students still rated them positively. It seems that as long as tutors are able to organise tutorials that meet students' expectations of enhancing their learning, they are ready to participate in a variety of more student-centred tutorial formats.

Flexibility in Learning

By far the most frequent issue raised related to the flexibility provided by distance learning for busy adults with family responsibilities, for example:

> *The distance learning mode is more convenient for busy working adults, such as teachers, because it does not require them to attend face-to-face sessions.*
>
> *It is very suitable for us because it gives us great freedom to schedule our work and study.*
>
> *One can plan one's study time to suit one's work requirements and family responsibilities.*
>
> *It is particularly useful for learners who are married and have children.*

Finally, perhaps it also needs to be recognised that distance learning may not be suitable for all learners. As one respondent said:

> *The distance learning mode of studying requires the learners to have high perseverance and analytical ability. If the learners do not have such qualities, it is better for them to attend more lectures or small group discussion.*

Concluding Comments

Overall, most students on the programme under review clearly valued the flexibility and freedom that distance education systems offer to busy adults. They also considered the materials to be well-produced, and of relevance to their day-to-day practice and professional development, and felt that they had matured into more independent learners.

It is recognised that the data above do not include direct observation of teachers' classroom activities, and that further research involving this dimension—for both distance *and* conventional in-service programmes—is sorely needed to arrive at any firm conclusions about the relative effectiveness of the two approaches.

Further evaluation activities are planned in relation to the programme under consideration, for example:

> asking a sample of students to keep a teaching portfolio, including a detailed account and review of a sequence of lessons;

followed by:

> semi-structured interviews which explore more fully the reasons for the strategies adopted.[4]

However, even on the basis of the results from the questionnaires noted above, it appears that many of the original doubts in Hong Kong about this form of delivery for teacher education were unjustified. Distance education programmes that are well designed and implemented—with materials of quality, in both content and pedagogy, allied to a comprehensive support system for learners—can provide an effective parallel system to the traditional provision for upgrading teachers.

The sorts of criticisms of distance education voiced in Hong Kong in the early 1990s are more muted now. This has arisen in part from a more widespread understanding among local educators of what this approach to teaching and learning involves; after all a substantial number of staff from other Hong Kong institutions have been employed by the OUHK in a wide of range of capacities, such as course developers, external assessors and external examiners. It reflects also an increasing convergence between distance and conventional models (Tait and Mills, 1999), driven particularly by the utilising of new technologies for teaching and learning in both systems and the Hong Kong government's commitment to lifelong learning policies (Education Commission, 2000).

Notes and References

1. The Education Commission is an advisory body on educational policy-making, and reports directly to the Chief Executive of Hong Kong.
2. The OLI was upgraded to University status in 1997. For simplicity, the University title is used for the most part in this article.
3. This date has since been brought forward to 2001.
4. Also, it may be of interest that other work has been carried out, albeit on a wider sample of students from several OUHK Education programmes, which has shown that a substantial number of the students interviewed had reached higher levels in their conceptions of learning and teaching during a year of study (Tang, 2000).

Correspondence

Ronnie Carr, School of Education and Languages, The Open University of Hong Kong, 30 Good Shepherd Street, Ho Man Tin, Kowloon, Hong Kong (rcarr@ouhk.edu.hk).

References

Brophy, M. and Dudley, B. (1981), Evaluation of Distance Teaching: A Criterion.

Sampling Approach in F. Percival and H. Ellington (Eds), *Distance Learning and Evaluation,* London: Kogan Page.

Brophy, M. and Dudley, B. (1982), Patterns of Distance Teaching in Teacher Education, *Journal of Education for Teaching,* 8, pp. 156-62.

Brophy, M. and Dudley, B. (1983), Training Teachers in the Third World, *Teaching at a Distance,* 23, pp. 40-45.

Chan, S.K. (1994), Students' Attitudes to Text Design and Face-to-Face Contact at the OLI Hong Kong, *Open Learning,* 9(2), pp. 51-53.

Coldevin, G. and Naidu, S. (1989), In-service Teacher Education at a Distance: Trends in Third World Development, *Open Learning,* 4(1), pp. 9-15.

Day, C. (1999), *Developing Teachers: The challenges of lifelong learning.* London: Falmer Press.

Education Commission (1992), *Education Commission Report No. 5,* Hong Kong: Government Printer.

Education Commission (2000), *Learning for Life: Learning through life,* Hong Kong: Printing Department.

Evans, T. and Nation, D. (1991), Distance Education and Teachers' Professional Development', in P. Hughes (Ed.) *Teachers' Professional Development,* Victoria: ACER.

Evans, T. and Nation, D. (1993), Educating Teachers at a Distance in Australia: Some trends, in H. Perraton (Ed.) *Distance Education for Teacher Training,* London: Routledge.

Fung, Y.H. and Carr, R. (1999), Tutorials in a Distance Education System: Students' expectations and preferred approaches, in R. Carr, O. Jegede, T.M. Wong and K.S. Yuen (Eds) *The Asian Distance Learner,* Hong Kong: Open University of Hong Kong Press.

Fung, Y. and Carr, R. (2000), Face-to-face Tutorials in a Distance Learning System: Meeting student needs, *Open Learning,* 15(1), pp. 35-46.

Garrison, D.R. (1993), A Cognitive Constructivist View of Distance Education: An analysis of teaching-learning assumptions, *Distance Education,* 14, 199-211.

Hargreaves, A. (1995), Development and Desire: A post-modern perspective, in T.R. Guskey and M. Huberman (Eds) *Professional Development in Education: New Paradigms and Practices,* New York: Teachers' College Press.

Holmberg, B. (1989), *Theory and Practice of Distance Education.* London: Routledge.

Holmes, D.R., Kermacharya, D.M. and Mayo, J.K. (1993), Radio Education in Nepal, in H. Perraton (Ed.), *Distance Education for Teacher Training.* London: Routledge.

Jarvis, P. (1997), Learning Practical Knowledge, in L. Kydd, M. Crawford and C. Riches (Eds), *Professional Development for Educational Management,* Buckingham: Open University Press.

Llewellyn, J., Hancock, G., Kirst, M. and Roeloffs, K. (1982), *A Perspective on Education in Hong Kong,* Hong Kong: Government Printer.

Mahlck, L. and Ternu, E.B. (1989), *Distance Versus College Trained Primary School Teachers: A case study from Tanzania,* Paris: International Institute for Educational Planning.

Mobida, M. (1997), Distance Teacher Education in South Africa: A critical analysis of pedagogical assumptions, *Teaching and Teacher Education,* 13, pp. 727-39.

Morgan, A.R. (1995), Student Learning and Students' Experiences: Research, theory and practice, in F. Lockwood (Ed.) *Open and Distance Learning Today,* London: Routledge.

Murphy, D. (1987), Offshore Education: A Hong Kong perspective, *Australian Universities Review,* 30(2), pp. 43-44.

Nielsen, H.D. and Tatto, M.T. (1991), *The Cost-effectiveness of Distance Education for Teacher Training,* BRIDGES Research Report Series, No. 9, Harvard: Harvard University Institute for International Development and the Harvard Graduate School of Education for USAID Bureau of Science and Technology.

Perraton, H. (1984), *Training Teachers at a Distance,* London: Commonwealth Secretariat.

Perraton, H. (Ed.) (1993), *Distance Education for Teacher Training.* London: Routledge.

Prescott, W. and Robinson, B., Teacher Education at the Open University, in

H. Perraton (Ed.) (1993), *Distance Education for Teacher Training*. London: Routledge.

Robinson, B. (1933), The Primary Teachers' Orientation Course, Allama Iqbal Open University, in H. Perraton (Ed.), *Distance Education for Teacher Training*, London: Routledge.

Rowntree, D. (1992), *Exploring Open and Distance Learning*. London, Kogan Page.

Rumble, G. (1997), *The Costs and Economics of Open and Distance Education.* London: Kogan Page.

Tait, A. and Mills, R. (1999), *The Convergence of Distance and Conventional Education*, New York: Routledge.

Tang, T.K.W. (2000), Conceptions of Teaching and Learning: Their relationship and variation over in-service teacher education, in D.A. Watkins and J.B. Biggs (Eds), *The Chinese Teacher.* Hong Kong: Comparative Education Research Centre, University of Hong Kong and Australian Council for Educational Research Ltd.

Yinger, R. and Hendricks-Lee, M. (1993), Working Knowledge in Teaching, in C. Day, J. Calderhead and P. Denicolo (Eds), *Research on Teacher Thinking: Understanding professional development*. London: Falmer Press.

APPENDIX IV

Distance Education in the E-9 Countries: India

India

The World Declaration on Education for All and the Framework for Action to meet Basic Learning Needs (Jomtien, 1990) were considered by the Indian Central Advisory Board of Education as a reaffirmation of their existing policy orientation given to elementary education in the National Policy on Education in 1986 (UNESCO, 2000, p. 9). These goals were incorporated into successive five-year plan proposals, the ninth five-year plan which operates from 1997-2002. India has therefore integrated EFA objectives into a policy framework which guides all educational initiatives at the state level. There were five main EFA challenges: (1) access to basic education for unreached sections of the population, (2) more community participation in education, (3) effective management structures, (4) improvement in the quality of formal systems through innovative teacher education programmes, and (5) a National Literacy Mission with a target of making more than 100 million in the 15-35 age group literate by 1999.

The government adopted particular strategies to achieve these goals, including a greater involvement of non-governmental organisations in non-formal community education programmes. This was also part of general move towards decentralisation of planning and management to make provision more responsive to local needs. The government also raised the percentage of public expenditure on education to 6 per cent. Another strategy was to attempt to create better links and integration between pre-school, primary education, non-formal education and adult education as well as integrating general healthcare and environmental issues into a broader spread of educational programmes.

Distance Education Projects

In the 1990s, there was a significant expansion of non-formal education (NFE), which in India covers out-of-school children and adult education. In 1997 there were 279,000 NFE centres educating 7 million people in 21 states. Most—some 241,000—are run by the state but some 86 per cent (38,000) are run by 544 non-governmental organisations or voluntary agencies.

One commonality amongst this wide range of educational providers is the flexible nature of the programmes they offer—condensed and part-time courses, village community locations and decentralised management. This flexibility is geared to accommodate local needs such as child labour and family duties and is designed to provide education that is equivalent to, though not the same as, that offered in formal settings. The certification of these programmes provides an entrance route into formal education.

One large-scale example is the *National Open School* (NOS) now renamed as National Institute of Open Learning (NIOS) which provides an alternative route to schooling for disadvantaged groups such as women and girls, scheduled castes and tribes, rural and urban poor and the unemployed. The school offers four different types of self-instructional programmes in English and Hindi: secondary, senior secondary (10-12th grade) bridge course (around grade 8) and vocational courses (free-standing or combined with academic courses).

A NOS student at the secondary level can choose home science and business studies, in addition to Mathematics, Science, English, Social Studies, or Bakery and Confectionery. At the senior-secondary levels, a student may choose subjects, such as political science, chemistry, or furniture and cabinet making. The learning resources are made available in the form of printed self-learning materials and magazines, personal contact programmes (PCPs), audio and video programmes and some television broadcasting. The courses are offered in English and a variety of local languages.

There are no formal entry requirements for the NOS programmes (except at senior-secondary level) and the range of courses and freedom to select is often better than in many schools.

The courses are distributed to students who attend classes or Personal Contact Programmes at study centres, generally within a regular school. Thus the OJS benefits from an existing school network to serve its students and enriches it by bringing in facilities not normally available to the schools

By 1998-99, NOS had 1,030 study centres, 812 Accredited Institutions (AIs), 14 Special Accredited Institutions for the Education of the Disadvantaged (SAIED), 204 Accredited Vocational Institutions (AVIs) and 8 regional centres. Annual enrolment grew from 34,800 in 1991—22 to 130,000 in 1998-99 with 61 per cent of students following secondary courses and 37 per cent of senior secondary courses. When compared to the 68 million in formal secondary school in 1996, this enrolment seems insubstantial (0.6 per cent of learners). Nevertheless, the chairman, speaking in 1995, predicted that open school methods would be used to reach 40 million students in sixteen languages within ten years.

Recent OJS completion rates were 26 per cent of junior secondary and 23 per cent of senior secondary but this compares to 70 per cent and 76 per cent in regular schools. The gender proportion within NOS is biased towards males (62.7 per cent *versus* 37.3 per cent). 33 per cent of their enrolments come from marginalised groups.

The Open School's income is derived from students' fees and the sale of books and materials. Currently learners pay 200 Rupees (Rps) (US$ 4.40) for the Foundation course, Rps 800 (US$ 18) for the Secondary course, and Rps 925 (US$ 21.28) for the Senior Secondary course. There are concessionary fees for handicapped students, ex-servicemen and members of scheduled castes and scheduled tribes. The cost per learner is US$ 10 and per graduate US$ 92. This compares to a cost par learner of US$ 40 in formal primary and US$ 44 in formal secondary (Edirisingha, 2000, p. 10).

At the moment NOS works from the lower secondary level but now proposes to introduce the *Open Elementary Education programmes* for out-of-school children of school-going age. The NOS has also recently launched the *Open Basic Education Project* at primary and upper primary level which will create a progression route into school education through the open schooling channel. There are three levels—preparatory (A), primary (B) and elementary (C), which are equivalent to formal school standards III, V and VIII. NOS is also planning the development of special education schooling and developing computer networking links between existing open schools. It is also producing open learning materials in the area of Education in Human Values for teachers involved in the Personal Contact Programme of NOS. This is for two types of teacher: those handling junior and senior secondary and those involved with non-governmental organisations. The materials consist of comic books, self-instructional print material and video-cassettes. The dedicated television channel of Gyan Darshan is also used for the broadcasting of visual materials and negotiations are being initiated with All India Radio for broadcasting of the audio-materials.

As part of the *Special Orientation for Primary Teachers* programme, the National Council for Educational Research and Training (NCERT), The Indira Gandhi National Open University (IGNOU) and the Indian Space Research Organisation have initiated several in-service teaching training courses using interactive video technology. Studio-based educators make live one-way video presentations about different teaching areas—aided by pre-recorded video-clips—to groups of teachers in different sites. These teachers engage in the particular subject area both before and after the broadcast through print materials and activities produced centrally by the twenty-strong course team but mediated at the local level by trained facilitators. Activity sheets are produced in the language of the participants. The teachers can ask direct questions to the educators through telephone and fax links. The approach uses satellite transmission for the one-way video and two-way audio interaction, the production of video-clips, computer systems, cable television, telephone and radio and television broadcasts.

In 1996 in Karnataka State, NCERT ran three seven-day pilot training courses for primary school teachers in 20 different district training institutes. In all, 300 teachers and 255 locally-based facilitators took part in the project. The second took place in Madhya Pradesh at 45 district training institutes. There was a third pilot in Karnataka aimed exclusively at Mathematics teachers that included help with teaching mathematics and to improving the trainees' knowledge of the subject. The fourth pilot ran courses for teacher facilitators in all the District Institutes of Education.

Achievements

One substantial factor in educational achievement in India was a change in the pattern of expenditure in education. There was a significant shift in the proportion of funds spent on elementary education in comparison to secondary and tertiary education. Within that funding a large proportion went towards expanding and improving school infrastructure, the recruitment of new teachers and teaching supplies.

A third of the world's non-literate people live in India—200 million in 1991, the majority of whom are female and living in rural areas. Nevertheless, India succeeded in raising the level of literacy in the "EFA decade" (1990-2000) from 52 per cent in 1991 to 64 per cent in 1997. This also included an 11 per cent rise in female literacy, compared to 9 per cent among males.

150 million children in the 6-14 age group were enrolled in school during the decade. This represented a 90 per cent enrolment rate. There was also a substantial expansion of primary and upper primary schools. 27,000 new schools were established between 1991-92 and 1996-97, leaving only 6 per cent of the rural population living more than one kilometre from a school. Under a programme called the *Education Guarantee Scheme* (EGS), the Indian government guaranteed to provide a school for any community with at least 25 school-age children. Of the 19,289 schools that were created under EGS up to September 1998, 10,325 (54 per cent) were in tribal areas and reflected successful targeting of socially deprived groups.

The number of teachers increased during the decade to at least two teachers per primary school. Between 1990-91 the number of teachers in the lower primary levels grew from 616.020 (85.25 per cent trained to required levels, 29.24 per cent of them female) to 1,871,542 (87 per cent trained and 34.34 per cent female). In the upper primary school level, the numbers grew from 1,072,911 (88.02 per cent trained and 33.24 per cent female) to 1,211,803 (88 per cent trained and 36.08 per cent female).

Challenges

India's rising population and massive number of illiterate people remain daunting challenges. Now that the population has crossed the one billion mark, trying to make the literacy rate keep pace with the population growth rate will become an unmanageable task. The rising population sets up an increasing demand for schools and creates difficulties in overcoming what are becoming entrenched disparities between rural and urban areas, different social groups and among different geographical regions.

Future Plans for Development in EFA Areas

The New National Campaign for EFA has set new targets for the coming decade: (1) access to EFA children age 6-14 by 2003; (2) completion of five years of primary education by all children by 2007; (3) completion of eight years of elementary education by all children by 2010. As a result, the Indian government has pledged that a greater emphasis will be placed on introducing the concept of inclusive schooling into both regular schools and the distance mode. Groups singled out for special attention are those who have proved difficult to include in significant numbers and those who have remained outside the formal and non-formal network. These include women and girls, scheduled castes and tribes, working children, children with disabilities, children from minority groups and urban disadvantaged children.

One strategy to achieve this will be the promotion of alternative delivery systems—seasonal, voluntary, open school and camp-type teaching approaches for special groups. These will need to be accompanied by appropriate teacher training courses. Another future area for development is the improvement of management systems in basic education, with a particular emphasis on greater co-ordination in planning and convergence between the different providers. This will involve an increased role for non-governmental organisations.

The enrolment capacity of the open-learning system is to be expanded to bring vocational and academic opportunities to a wider section of the population. This will include a bigger focus on adult literacy programmes and ones that link in with established non-formal provision. Early childhood care and education is to be expanded and there is to be a focus on the improvement of quality in schools by investing in their infrastructure, expanding pre- and in-service teacher education and reviewing the content and methodology of teaching.

TABLE I

Major Distance Education Projects in India

Audience/Purpose	*Project/Institution*	*Date*	*Scale*	*Outcomes*
Out-of-school and marginalised children and adolescents	*Open elementary education (National Open School)*	NA	NA	New equivalency programme for out-of-school children.
Adult basic education *(equivalence programmes and non-formal education)*	*The National Open School (NOS)*	1989	130,000 enrolled in 1998-99 from most states and Union Territories in India. 900 study centres, 8 regional centres.	Learner-selected courses in academic and vocational subjects at foundation, junior and senior-secondary levels. Targeting disadvantaged groups aged 14-89, the majority 18-24. NOS launched study centres in the Middle East, i.e. Dubai and Abu Dhabi. 6.5 million books produced in 1998-99. 140,796 certified students at junior-secondary level in 1998. Cost per learner US$ 10[b].
	Open Basic Education Project	1999		Equivalency programme for adults.

Teacher education	*NCERT's Special Orientation for Primary Teachers Programme and Programme of Mass Orientation of School Teachers*	1998	3,000 primary teachers. 255 facilitators	Teleconferencing teacher-training programme using interactive video technology. Gives remote teachers access to a panel of specialist educators who make presentations about different teaching areas. Study group activities precede and follow broadcast. 7-day courses, 13 thematic areas explored. Achievement tests showed gains in skills[c].
	Diploma in Primary Education, Indira Gandhi National Open University (IGNOU)	NA	NA	In-service training
	Bombay Television Centre	NA	NA	20-min. programme, once a week, aim at improving knowledge and skills[c].
	Hints for Teachers Notional TV	NA	NA	One 45-min broadcast a week raising awareness of innovations in teaching.

Sources: a UNESCO, 2000; b Edirisingha, 2000, p. 10; c Perraton and Creed, 1999, p. 55.

APPENDIX V

Revised Schemes of the Teacher Education in India

Revision of the Scheme During XI Plan

The proposal of Department of School Education & Literacy, Ministry of Human Resource Development for revision and expansion of the Centrally Sponsored Scheme of Teacher Education during the XI Plan was considered by Expenditure Finance Committee (EFC) at its meeting held on 13th November, 2007. EFC recommended comprehensive evaluation of the Teacher Education Scheme. Till such evaluation, the existing Scheme of Teacher Education may continue without any change in its existing norms and parameters. National Council for Educational Research & Training (NCERT) has been entrusted with the task to evaluate the Teacher Education Scheme.

For the purpose of carrying out the evaluation, the NCERT and its team of experts will be undertaking visits to the state governments, SCERTs and the various teacher training institutions (TTIs) of the country to obtain 'first hand' knowledge of the functioning of the TTIs. In the process, they would also be interacting with the various stakeholders. The state governments may extend full cooperation to the visiting teams. At the same time, if the state governments/SCERTs have any suggestions which would be useful in evaluating the Scheme and in modifying the existing guidelines on Teacher Education, the same may be forwarded to the Ministry at the earliest, so that the same could be considered in the evaluation process.

Background of the Centrally Sponsored Scheme on Teacher Education

Original Scheme

As envisaged in the National Policy on Education (NPE), 1986, and its Programme of Action (POA), a Centrally-Sponsored Scheme of Restructuring and Reorganization of Teacher Education was launched in 1987 to create a sound institutional infrastructure for pre-service and in-service training of elementary & secondary school teachers and for provision of academic resource support to elementary and secondary schools. The Scheme had, inter alia, the following component:

(i) Setting up of District Institutes of Education and Training (DIETs);
(ii) Strengthening of Secondary Teachers Education Institutions into Colleges of Teacher Education (CTEs) and Institutes of Advanced Study in Education (IASEs);
(iii) Strengthening of State Councils of Educational Research and Training (SCERTs);

Revised Scheme Under Xth Five Year Plan

The Scheme was revised under the Xth Plan, with the following main objectives:

1. Speedy completion of DIET/CTE/IASE/SCERT projects, which have been sanctioned but not completed up to the end of the IX Plan period.
2. Making DIETs, CTEs, IASEs sanctioned (and SCERTs strengthened) upto the IX Plan period, optimally functional and operational.
3. Sanction and implementation of fresh DIET/CTE/IASE/SCERT projects to the extent necessary.
4. Improvement in the quality of programmes being undertaken by DIETs, etc. especially those of pre-service and in-service training, so as to enable them to effectively play their nodal role of improving quality of elementary and secondary education in their respective jurisdiction, as measured in terms of levels of learner achievement.

Background

There has been a phenomenal growth of teaching profession in India since independence. During 1994-95, about 4.3 million teachers were working in different levels of schools. Of these, 2.7 million (66 per cent) were engaged in primary and upper primary schools. Between the period 1990 to 1995, the total strength of teachers at different levels of school education increased from 4.0 million to nearly 4.7 million, marking an increase of 7.5 per cent. If this trend continues, the number of teachers, particularly primary and upper primary teachers will grow significantly over the next decade. A sex-wise analysis of the teacher force indicates that there are more male teachers than female teachers at all levels of school education. Although the number of female teachers has increased, yet their share in total teaching force is small, particularly, in rural, remote and educationally backward areas. The percentage of women teachers in schools increased from 29.4 per cent in 1987-88 to 32.08 per cent in 1993-94.

A fully qualified primary teacher as recommended by the National Policy on Education, 1986, is expected to have twelve years of schools education followed by two years of primary teacher training. However, the practice differs from state to state. There are teachers with ten years of general education and one year of primary teacher training. A large number of teachers recruited before 1986 have had ten years of general education. There are teachers, usually very senior, who have eight years or less of general education. While data on teachers' pre-qualification is not adequate, it is estimated that there are about 0.24 million teachers who are not fully qualified.

The National Policy on Education, 1986, and also as revised in 1992, placed significant emphasis on pre-induction training as well as on in-service continuing education of primary teachers. Over the years, India has developed a multi-tier infrastructure for teacher education. At the national level, National Council of Education Research and Training (NCERT), set-up in 1961, leads the county in designing exemplar instructional material on teacher education and providing training through innovative programmes. National Council for Teacher Education (NCTE) was set-up in August 1995 under an Act of Parliament for planned and co-ordinated development of teacher education. Indira Gandhi

National Open University (IGNOU), through its School of Education offers teacher education programmes in the distance mode. State Councils of Educational Research and Training (SCERTs) were set-up in 20 states and State Institutes of Education (SIEs) in nine other states as the state counterpart of the NCERT to provide direction and leadership to reforms in school education including teacher education. Below the state level there are elementary teacher training institutions which are continuously being upgraded since 1987 under a Centrally Sponsored Scheme (CSS).

Teacher Education Scheme

As envisaged in the National Policy on Education, the Centrally Sponsored Scheme of Restructuring and Reorganization of Teacher Education was taken up in 1987 to create a viable institutional infrastructure, academic and technical resource base for orientation, training and continuous upgradation of knowledge, competence and pedagogical skills of elementary school teachers in the country. The scheme has the following five components:

- Setting up of District Institutes of Education and Training (DIETs) to organise pre-service and in-service courses for elementary school teachers and for personnel working in non-formal and adult education.
- Strengthening of Colleges of Teacher Education (CTEs) and development of about 50 of them as Institutes of Advance Study in Education (IASEs).
- Revitalization of State Councils of Education Research and Training (SCERTs).
- Mass Orientation of school teachers under a planned programme to be implemented under the supervision of NCERT.
- Establishment and Strengthening of Departments of Education in the Universities through Universities Grants Commission (UGC).

Establishment of DIETs under Centrally Sponsored Scheme of Teacher Education is a major intervention as there did not exist facilities for continuous Teacher Education at district level before the launch of this Scheme. It has been envisaged that DIETs would provide for training and resource support to Elementary Education (both formal and non-formal) and Adult Education systems at the grass-root level. A DIET has three main functions:

- Training both induction level as well as in-service.
- Resource support extension/guidance, development of materials, teaching aids, evaluation tools, etc.
- Action research.

All programmes of pre-service and in-service teacher education are so designed as to train the teacher/instructor in transacting curriculum, keeping the learner at the centre of the teaching-learning process.

DIETs have been established throughout the country either by upgradation of the existing Primary Teachers Training Institutions (PTTIs) or by establishment of a completely new district level institution. In both the cases central assistance is provided for either upgrading the existing physical infrastructure of a PTTI or for setting up of a new building with adequate facilities of class rooms, hostels, administrative block and staff quarters. As per the norms approved for the VIIIth Plan, non-recurring assistance up to Rs. 5.8 million could be sanctioned for additional civil work of an upgraded DIET and up to Rs. 10 million for a completely new building. Besides this, an amount up to Rs. 1.7 million could be sanctioned for procurement of necessary equipment and other teaching aids. As far as recurring assistance is concerned, the central government undertakes to reimburse the full expenditure on pay and allowances of faculty (31) and administrative staff (17) sanctioned for various DIETs along with the expenditure incurred on training programmes and contingencies. By the end of last financial year (31st March 1999) 451 DIETs have been established/upgraded, out of which 380 are operational and organizing training programmes.

The Secondary stage is a vital one in the educational system. It is the terminal stage of school education which prepares students either for higher education or for going into a vocation of their choice. With the introduction of the 10+2 system throughout the country and the objective of introducing vocational courses at the +2 stage, secondary stage of the school system has acquired an even greater significance, and so naturally has the education of secondary school teachers. With the setting up of District Institutes of Education and Training for elementary school teachers, it also became necessary to produce good quality elementary teacher educators. Thus selected secondary teacher education institutions combined twin functions of education of secondary school teachers as well as of elementary teacher educators. The system of secondary teacher education, therefore performs the following broad functions:

- Imparting of quality pre-service and in-service education to the secondary school teachers;
- Preparation of personnel for the faculties of elementary teacher education institutions, and their continuing education;
- Provision of general resource support to the secondary schools and elementary teacher education institutions; and
- Research, innovation and extension work in the field of secondary education and elementary teacher education.

To facilitate the training of secondary level teachers and teachers educators of DIETs, 76 Colleges of Teacher Education (CTEs) and 34 Institutes of Advanced Studies in Education (IASEs) have been set-up throughout the country under teacher education scheme. In all about 2600 teacher training institutions are functioning both in government and private sectors which provide pre-service and in-service training to teachers and teacher educators.

Strengthening of State Councils of Educational Research and Training (SCERTs) is an important component of teacher education scheme. These councils are expected to perform multifarious role and responsibilities relating to research, development, training, extension, documentation and consultancy. Though majority of States have established these councils the status of most of them requires upgradation in terms of better infrastructure and faculty to enable them to come up to the level of vibrant state level organisations, capable of playing an effective role as lead institutions. Efforts are on to make the state level institutions autonomous and independent with over all responsibilities to supervise and guide functioning of DIETs, CTEs and other teacher education institutions in the state.

The National Council for Teacher Education (NCTE) has been established as a National level statutory body by the Government of India in August, 1995 with the objectives of achieving planned and coordinated development of teacher education system, regulation and proper maintenance of norms and standards of teacher education and for matters connected therewith. Some of its major functions are laying down norms for various teacher education courses, recognition of teacher education institutions, laying down guidelines in respect of minimum qualifications for appointment of teachers, surveys and studies, research and innovations and prevention of commercialisation of teacher education. As per the provisions of the NCTE Act, four Regional Committees for the Northern, Southern, Eastern and Western regions have been set-up at Jaipur, Bangalore, Bhubaneshwar and Bhopal respectively. These Regional Committees consider the applications of institutions of teacher education for recognition/ permission in accordance with the provisions of the NCTE Act. The Council has laid down norms and standards for pre-primary, elementary and secondary level teacher education institutions and for B.Ed. course through correspondence/distance education mode. Besides a number of useful publications on the subject of teacher education, a new curriculum Framework on Teacher Education has recently been brought by the Council.

Some of the Innovative Interventions in Teacher Education

Shiksha Karmi Project

Shiksha Karmi Project (SKP) is being implemented in Rajasthan since 1987 with assistance from Swedish International Development Co-operation Agency (SIDA). The project aims at Universalisation and qualitative improvement of primary education in remote and socio-economically backward villages in Rajasthan with primary attention to girls. The project identifies teacher absenteeism as a major obstacle in achieving the goal of

Universalisation of Elementary Education (UEE). It was realised that a primary school in remote villages, with the teacher not residing there, often tended to become dysfunctional, and parents as well as children failed to relate to such an institution, leading to high drop-out rates. Under SKP, regular teachers are replaced by local teachers who are less qualified but specially trained. The Shiksha Karmi (SK) is a local person with minimum educational qualification of Class VIII for men and Class V for women. To overcome the basic lack of qualification, Shiksha Karmis are given intensive training through induction programme as well as periodic refresher courses. Shiksha Karmi Project (SKP) is being implemented in Rajasthan since 1987 with assistance from Swedish International Development Co-operation Agency (SIDA). The project aims at Universalisation and qualitative improvement of primary education in remote and socio-economically backward villages in Rajasthan with primary attention to girls. The project identifies teacher absenteeism as a major obstacle in achieving the goal of Universalisation of Elementary Education (UEE). It was realised that a primary school in remote villages, with the teacher not residing there, often tended to become dysfunctional, and parents as well as children failed to relate to such an institution, leading to high drop-out rates. Under SKP, regular teachers are replaced by local teachers who are less qualified but specially trained. The Shiksha Karmi (SK) is a local person with minimum educational qualification of Class VIII for men and Class V for women. To overcome the basic lack of qualification, Shiksha Karmis are given intensive training through induction programme as well as periodic refresher courses.

Major achievements under Shiksha Karmi Projects are as follows:

- A six-fold increase in enrolment of children in the age group of 6-14 years in Shiksha Karmi Schools and Prehar pathshalas (School of convenient timings).
- Enrolment of children in the age group 6-14 years in primary education in SKP villages has improved significantly from 37% to 83% at present
- Enrolment of boys has gone up from 50% to 93% enrolment of girls has increased from 21% to 76%.

- Monthly attendance of children in SK schools has improved from 58% to 84%.
- Retention of children in schools which have been with the project for more than five year has improved considerably.
- 1979 disabled children have been integrated in SK schools.
- 55% of the children in SK schools belong to the Scheduled Castes and Scheduled Tribes and 19% to Other Backward Classes (OBCs).
- One of the outstanding achievements of SKP is 100% enrolment of children in the age group of 6-14 years in 576 villages i.e., more than one-fourth of project villages.
- The SKP has constituted 2600 Village Education Committees (VECs) in villages to promote community involvement in primary education and encourage village level planning, supervision and management in improving effectiveness of schools.
- A number of strategies have been tried out and implemented in the SKP for the promotion of girl education.
- Prehar Pathshalas have enabled out of school children, especially girls in the remote areas to avail of opportunities for primary schooling at their own pace and with sufficient flexibility. At present 22,138 girls who constitute 68% of learners in PPs are benefiting from this facility.
- Angan Pathshalas (Courtyard Schools) for small children, particularly girls who cannot travel long distances to attend schools, have been started. At present, 97 APS centers are in operation with 4023 children.
- In order to facilitate and increase the enrolment of girls in villages where literate women are not available to work as SKs, 14 Mahila Prakshikshan Kendras (Women Training Centers) have been set-up in interior rural areas in which 334 women are being trained.

MV Foundation Programme

MV Foundation programme is being run in the Ranga Reddy district of Andhra Pradesh for Universalisation of Elementary Education. It was started neither as a low-cost alternative to regular government teachers in schools, nor in response to teacher absenteeism. It has its origin in the organisation's concern for eradication of child labour. The MVF strategy is to release children from labour and put them into the regular government schools. The role of the para teacher, a local youth, is:

- To campaign against child labour,
- To mobilise children, parents and the community in favour of schooling,
- To run bridge courses for children released from labour for giving them basic literacy and numeracy skill and getting them used to the school life, and
- To assist the government teachers in teaching, and to retain the new entrants recently released from labour and put in to school after an intense campaign.

These para teachers have also helped in sensitising the government teachers to take a stand against child labour, and towards larger educational reforms, which is the MVF agenda. More than 1600 para teachers are active in Ranga Reddy district at present. The programme which started in 1991 has grown rapidly. It has already succeeded in putting 50,000 children back into schools.

Volunteer Teacher Scheme

The Himachal Pradesh Volunteer Teacher Scheme (HPVTS) was introduced by the state government of Himachal Pradesh in 1984. The HPVTS was formulated to provide an additional volunteer teacher to the single teacher primary school. This was needed because there was an increase in the enrolment in government schools. Further, the scheme was started to provide work to educated unemployed youth for a short period of time. After completion of 10 years service VTS are regularised as Junior Basic Teacher. The Teachers appointed under this scheme must live within a radius of 5 Km. of the single teacher primary school.

S/he receives points in the selection process for being local and his/her educational qualifications can range from The Himachal Pradesh Volunteer Teacher Scheme (HPVTS) was introduced by the state government of Himachal Pradesh in 1984. The HPVTS was formulated to provide an additional volunteer teacher to the single teacher primary school. This was needed because there was an increase in the enrolment in government schools. Further, the scheme was started to provide work to educated unemployed youth for a short period of time. After completion of 10 years service VTS are regularised as Junior Basic Teacher. The Teachers appointed under this scheme must live within a radius of 5 Km. of the single teacher primary school. S/he receives points in the selection process for being local and his/her educational qualifications can range from Matric to B.A./B.Ed. The candidates also undergo a personal interview and are awarded points based on their performance.

Action Plan to Increase Opportunities for Professional Development of Teachers—Introduction of Distance Mode in Teacher Training

Electronic media has a time-tested, large and definite role to play in the field of Distance Education. In fact, the latest innovations in the arena of teachers' training through distance education are based on electronic media. Educational Television is more than 35 years old in India. Educational Radio is still older. In terms of response of the students, it is in favour of educational television which broadcasts both image and voice. Teachers and students have graduated from pure audio to the image and voice learning media. Next logical step is two-way interaction—and expectation will be interaction with image and voice—preferably two-way video—otherwise at least one-way video and two-way audio.

Indira Gandhi National Open University (IGNOU), with a national jurisdiction, state of the art media production facilities, fairly well-established student support services and expertise in teacher education has been making attempts to provide teacher education/training packages for teachers in the institutions of higher education and primary education through distance education. With the aim to cater to the training needs of the primary sector, the School of Education, IGNOU went into a collaboration with National Council of Educational Research and Training (NCERT) in 1993. It is offering a Certificate Programme in Guidance for primary school teachers and parents and is in the process of developing a comprehensive programme titled "Diploma in Primary Education (DPE)", following a modular approach, for training the untrained primary school teachers in the North-Eastern States of India. There is also a plan to extend this programme in other State in subsequent years. The University makes use of self-instructional print materials, audio and video programmes, theoretical and activity-oriented assignments, tutorials and academic counselling, contact session and internship, Radio and TV broadcast and teleconferencing for its professional programmes.

At the Centre level, Government of India has funded a successful experimentation in introduction of distance education mode in delivering training packages to the primary teachers under the existing "Special Orientation Programme for Primary School Teachers"—a training programme with cascade model. This distance education mode has made use of the interactive video technology. Two pilot projects have been taken up by the implementing agency—the National Council of Educational Research and Training (NCERT). The first pilot project was taken up during January, 1996 in the state of Karnataka. 850 primary school teachers who had been assembled in 20 centres, were trained. The learning centres were almost at a distance of 2500 kms from the Teaching Centre. The seven day programme had 14 sessions, each of which was on various topics such as Minimum Levels of Learning, Teaching Aids, Mufti-Grade Teaching and strategies for teaching Mathematics, Environmental studies and Languages. Each of the sessions was of about 210 minutes (120 minutes of live interaction and 90 minutes of individual and group activities). Each session comprised of self-study, presentation and demonstration (live and pre-recorded) by experts, panel discussions, teachers interaction with panelists through telephone and fax and also group activities. NCERT's Central Institute of Technology (CIET) had also conducted a Classroom 2000+ experiment in May 1993 which demonstrated the potential of Interactive Video Technology in direct teaching of Physics and

Mathematics concepts to group of students spread at various distant locations in the country. It made use of Television set, a telephone and computer key pads for trainees making responses. The similar mode had now been tried for teacher training.

Keeping these developments in mind, India's National Action Plan (NAP) for In-service Education of Primary Teachers through Distance Education—a perspective plan to integrate all the ongoing programmes in this direction, has been prepared. In this plan it has been felt that only by pressing into service the distance education mode, equipped with modern training technology, it will be possible to provide in-service training to all primary teachers every year and their trainers and supervisors every second year. Thus the technology aspect has to play a big role in implementing this plan. Therefore, it has been also felt necessary to test-run yet another pilot project to train teachers through distance mode using interactive technology. With the collaboration from UNESCO and the International Telecommunication Union (ITU), Government of India has taken up a pilot programme on In-service Primary Teacher Training (IPTT) through application of interactive television (ITV) in distance education.

The project will aim at designing and pilot testing a continuing in-service education of primary teachers and teacher educators (DIET Staff). It will simultaneously validate and standardise technology specifications for interactive television system for application in distance education in the developing countries. The major objectives of the project are:

- to design and implement an interactive distance education programme for primary teachers and DIET staff throughout a wide geographical area in the selected States,
- develop print, audio and video software according to the requirements of the proposed distance education programme,
- to use interactive television (ITV) to improve quality of interactivity in distance education programme and standardise technology specifications for ITV for application in distance education,
- to gain insight into the organisational managerial and technical constraints and problems to interactive

distance education for in-service training of primary teachers, and consider the trade-off between large number of learners and the level/quality of interaction.

Some of the major outputs of this project will be standardisation of ITV technology for application in distance education; training of at least 8000 teachers and teacher trainers; gain of experience and insight during the implementation, learning centres would get equipped with reception facilities in addition to the existing educational technology aids and equipment. Strategically, this project will be built upon available programmes, experience and infrastructure. It does not propose training set-up *de-novo*. Another component of the strategy is to involve the State Governments and State level institutions in administrative and academic decision-making in the project. This is important, because, the training of primary teachers has to be dealt by the State governments and State agencies.

During the implementation phase, five one-week programmes each in two different Indian Languages (Gujarati and Hindi) will be held for teacher educators and teachers. These programmes will be carefully staggered so that each programme or a group of programmes are followed by intensive review and programme modifications. The five programmes in each language will be spread over 24 weeks of implementation allowing on an average four weeks of interim period for review and modifications—both from the angle of pedagogy as well as technological application. The ultimate beneficiaries of the project are the primary school students and hence, the country as a whole. Direct beneficiaries are the professional staff in the DIETs and the primary teachers. Interactivity will be the main feature of the programme delivery. Several levels of interactivity have been proposed. They are:

(a) Face-to-face interaction;
(b) Satellite-based interactive learning;
(c) Inter-centre information exchange; and
(d) Computer assisted interactive learning.

Special feature of the project will be experimentation with

alternative interactive modes at different locations. The learning Centres will comprise urban, semi-urban and rural sectors. Although the self-study and face-to-face interactions will remain the same in different learning centres, the return path of the ITV component will vary. Five centres each will have satellite based talk back facility, voice-mail, STD/FAX and data network. Subject to availability, a few Centres will use ISDN facility/video telephone. This will provide 3 × 4, i.e. 12 different modalities within the project for experimentation of effectiveness and cost-efficiency of different approaches.

APPENDIX VI

Media and Technology Uses in Teacher Education

In Table 1 we expand on this brief summary, identifying the strengths and weaknesses of a range of technologies for teacher education.

TABLE 1
Media and Technology Uses in Teacher Education

Function in Teacher Education and Development	*Strengths*	*Limitations and Requirements*
Print		
Provides information, concepts and examples in a structured way. Can teach academic subject content, education theory and knowledge about pedagogy. Can link subject knowledge to school curricula and teaching methods. Can combine expert input with teacher-produced materials. Can show teachers' lesson plans, extracts from teachers' diaries and accounts, diagrams of classroom or equipment layout and examples of pupils' work.	A learning resource in a permanent form, permitting individual or group use. A portable and convenient resource. Copies can be used by more than one teacher. Good for explaining theory and concepts and providing detailed information. Can include a variety of source materials. Can be low cost but scale affects costs. Provides a common standardised resource.	Physical distribution of the materials can be slow or difficult in some contexts. Fixed content, not quickly responsive to sudden changes in school curricula or educational legislation or teacher education curricula. Requires relatively lengthy preparation time and team-working by those producing the materials. Cannot show teaching-learning interaction at work in real time in classrooms. As a standardised resource, it may not meet the needs of minority groups or- languages, or regional variation.

(Contd.)

Function in Teacher Education and Development	Strengths	Limitations and Requirements
Can provide transcripts of teacher-pupil interaction for analysis. Can provide guides to action for teachers (e.g. in implementing new curricula or doing action research).	If well designed, can combine effectively with other media. Can play a variety of roles, from lead medium to supplementary resource.	A one-way medium. Interaction is possible with the material, with the school environment applying ideas from the materials, with other teachers in local groups or with tutors.
Radio		
Provides topical information and current news for teachers. Illustrates text content or addresses educational issues in a lively way, using authentic voices and varied sources (teachers, policy-makers, parents, curriculum developers, education experts). Can raise awareness about education in a wider community audience Offers a forum for teacher exchanges (teachers' voices). Can reach all or most teachers at the same time to support faster and more widespread information dissemination.	Often widely accessible by teachers Can be responsive to teachers' needs within a short time-scale. Provides immediacy in the materials can be very low cost per teacher. Equipment for production can be simple, relatively inexpensive and durable. Use of local radio can increase the relevance of programmes and respond to local needs or languages. Programmes can take a variety of formats and fulfil different purposes: a flexible medium. Can integrate effectively with print.	Ephemeral or impermanent, content lost unless recorded. Scheduled transmission times may as inconvenient. Has a poor and unglamorous image Needs teamwork and collaboration when integrated with other media (can be difficult to achieve in practice). Often limited by regulatory framework for broadcasting or lack of enabling policy for educational use. Commercialisation of radio increasing costs for production or transmission. Weak in conveying detailed or conceptually dense: material. One way medium.

Interactive Radio		
Provides well-structured lessons for teachers and pupils alike in a range of subjects. Compensates for weak teacher-knowledge and can improve it at the same time.	Has proved effective in several contexts for teaching English as a second language, maths and other subjects. Can reach a mass audience at relatively low cost per learner. Can support teachers in subject knowledge and in demonstrating new teaching methods. Structures active learning as part of the lesson. Can provide models of lessons.	Scheduling may be at inappropriate times. Depends on regular and reliable transmission facilities and broadcasting infrastructure. Cassette tapes can substitute but lose immediacy and need physical distribution, Needs skilled programme designers and structures for teacher support with training for them where interactive radio is new. A one-way medium. Interaction is with materials, with and between children in class and ideally with other teachers.
Audio-Cassette Tapes		
Provides illustrations through sound. Can give examples of concepts and theory. Can convey information. Can provide discussion in a more natural way than through text. Can provide detailed instructions (e.g. in using a computer or manipulating equipment). Can provide sequences of conversation for close analysis.	Offers a permanent resource for individuals or groups. Is relatively portable. Cassette players are often widely accessible by teachers .Can be re-played, stopped and started at will by learner. Combines effectively with print, and can extend the use of radio programmes through recording for re-play. Is low cost to develop and duplicate.	Audio-cassettes can deteriorate over time. Sound quality can be poor if a chain of recordings are made or if the equipment is poor. Cassettes need good management (e.g. accurate labelling, storing, mechanisms for circulating among teachers). Can fail to stimulate active learning if used just to deliver lectures. Tape-editing time often underestimated.

(Contd.)

Function in Teacher Education and Development	*Strengths*	*Limitations and Requirements*
Can be used as a teachers' 'talking newsletter'. Can provide models of pronunciation. Can act as a 'voice in the ear', to guide teachers through processes (e.g. learning to use a computer or observation tasks)	Can be a more intimate or motivating medium than print, if not presented as a single-voice long lecture. Provides good models in language learning and teaching, and sequences of natural conversation. Can demonstrate communicative approaches in language teaching. Teachers can contribute to tapes or make them. Can be used by tutors to give feedback to students.	Needs skilled integration with print or other media. Content often needs designing differently from radio programmes. A one-way medium.
CD-ROM (Compact Disk-Read Only Memory)		
Provides access to information for teachers in text, graphics, audio and video form. Can provide information on curricula content and teaching methods.	Can store large amounts of information on one disk. Relatively cheap and simple to copy and distribute. Provides random access to content, so a particular segment can be located without having to rewind as in audio-cassettes. Can substitute for lack of access to databases where computers lack connection to Internet.	Requires a computer with CD-ROM drive and software to access the disk. Stores less audio material than audio-cassette tapes. More expensive than audio-tapes. Making CD-ROM interactive increases development costs.

Television		
Can reach a mass audience of teachers and the community. Can raise awareness in the community at large about educational issues and teaching. Shows processes in real-time or slowed down or in close-up (e.g. classroom interaction, language development, mathematical operations). Shows a variety of school and classroom contexts and teachers in action which teachers would not otherwise see, given the isolated nature of teachers' work. Gives teachers comparisons and benchmarks. Can show specialists or experts at work. Provides material as the basis of group discussion.	Can demonstrate real contexts and provide rich visual content. Can capture classroom realities. Can combine a variety of content (e.g. bite visits to schools; interviews, dynamic simulations, and examples of teachers' work). Can be combined with other media. Can provide topical content.	High programme development costs and may be high transmission costs. But modest cost per viewer possible on large enough scale. Not always accessible to all teachers. Inadequate technical support at local level sometimes leaves non-functioning equipment. Often inappropriate transmission times for teachers. Sometimes replicates traditional lecture formats which fail to make effective use of the medium's capabilities. One-way medium. May foster passive viewing. Filming in schools requires considerable specialist skills and resources. Filming in studio classrooms is often easier but can lack authenticity.

(Contd.)

Function in Teacher Education and Development	*Strengths*	*Limitations and Requirements*
Video-Cassettes		
Shows processes in real-time or slowed down. Shows a variety of school and classroom contexts and teachers at work which the viewing teachers would not otherwise see. Can provide separate segments for close analysis relating to different parts of the course materials, not only long sequences. Commercially-produced video-cassettes, for example, on child development or other educational topics, can be 're-purposed' for particular educational uses (segments selected and printed guides produced in relation to them).	Can be relatively low cost, depending on development costs and scale of use. Has some of the strengths of television but can be used in different ways for learning (under the control of the learner who can stop, start and re-play sequences). Can provide material for close observation and analysis, if teacher is guided either on the cassette or in print. Can be used by individual teachers or groups. Can be combined with print. Is a permanent resource. It can support active learning with good instructional design; demonstrate teachers' beliefs and practices; stimulate discussion; show the realities of teaching in different schools and compensate for teachers' lack of access to other schools; show simulations and role play (e.g. in head-teacher training) or children's work.	Requires physical distribution of video-cassettes and access to playback facilities convenient for teachers. Quality (picture and sound) can deteriorate if copies of copies are made rather than from the master tape. The cassettes need good management (accurate labelling, storing, mechanisms for circulation). Their role needs to be carefully designed to embed them in the course materials or in relation to active learning, if they are not to be a marginal resource. Video may be poor technical quality (poor lighting and sound, one camera recording only the teacher (not the children) and poor educational quality (e.g. presentation of whole 45 minute lesson). Editing time is often underestimated. Needs professional makers to achieve good quality.

Video Use in Micro-Teaching		
Provides a means for student-teachers, to observe themselves on recorded video in a teaching situation or simulation, and to get feedback on their performance through viewing the video and discussion with tutor and peers. Provides student-teachers with an opportunity for observing, interpreting and discussing the video material. Provides opportunities for observing and comparing the performance of self with others.	Is effective up to a point, in assisting student-teachers to appraise their own and others' performance and assist the initiation of reflective practice. Provides opportunities for practice and experiment followed by feedback; helps the student-teacher develop specific skills (such as questioning, explaining, managing time-on-task, setting up group-work, using a particular teaching method). A short amount of recording can generate a large amount of discussion and analysis (5-10 minutes of recording can generate at least an hour of analysis and feedback) with a skilled tutor. Gives attention to the individual student-teacher.	Is labour-intensive and small scale, therefore relatively high cost as a form of face-to-face teaching. Effectiveness depends on the quality of the tutor or facilitator, the preparation by tutor and student-teacher, the tutor's skill in facilitate and timing of feedback. Has been criticises as concentrating on isolated, decontextualised and specific teaching skills or competences rather than deep understanding. Requires a room to be set-up appropriately as a classroom, with adequate lighting and equipment but can be relatively low-cost to set-up. More difficult to do over a distance.
Audio Tele-Conferencing		
Enables real-time interaction among teachers and educators in different locations. Can bring together teachers, curriculum developers, specialists and policy-makers in one event.	Can support development of teachers across large distances, enabling contact between groups. Is relatively easy to use (no large amount of technical know-how to master).	Facilitating group discussion across a number of sites needs high levels of skills and preparation. Requires advance organisation, scheduling and coordination to make the event successful.

(Contd.)

Function in Teacher Education and Development	*Strengths*	*Limitations and Requirements*
Can be used for presentations and teaching sessions, discussions, course delivery (in combination with other media) and student support.	Can be cost effective but depends on context and comparisons with alternatives. Can provide topical content at short notice more easily than print (has the immediacy (or more) of radio). Can be combined with video-conferencing (one-way video, two-way audio) to reduce video-conferencing costs and to provide interactivity where the infrastructure or budget does not support two-way video-conferencing.	Special equipment needed so that learners usually have to travel to venue. Costs vary in different countries, but can be cost effective when compared with alternatives. Requires adequate telecommunications infrastructure to function and ensure adequate sound quality. Requires additional materials or two-way graphics for some topics and subjects.
Video-Conferencing		
[rabies real-time interaction among teachers and educators in different locations. Can bring together teachers, curriculum developers, specialists and policy-makers in one event. Can be used for presentations and teaching sessions, discussions, course delivery (in combination with other media) and student support. Can show a variety of visual materials to participants.	Can support development of teachers across large distances, enabling contact between groups. Can provide topical content at short notice more easily than print (has the immediacy or more) of radio). Can make scarce expertise available widely.	Has high start-up costs; usage levels need to be high enough to recover them. Requires technical support, including at remote sites. Requires students to travel to venue; give the cost of equipping sites, these are likely to be less local than options using different technologies. Where teacher interaction is possible at the local or district level, video-conferencing is likely to be a more expensive option.

		Where teachers travel long distances to in-service events, the video-conferencing option may be more cost-effective. The added costs of the visual dimension may not provide matching benefits over audio-alone.
Computers		
Provides access to information on CD-ROM and local databases. A means of preparing materials for teaching if consumables are available (e.g. cartridges, paper). Provides computer-based learning materials for teachers and pupils.	Can provide access to large amounts of resources for teachers to select from and use as appropriate in their own contexts or for their own development. Its use helps teachers to develop their own personal computer skills.	The quality of software or learning programmes is sometimes poor. Technical support is needed and may be scarce in rural areas. Access is sometimes restricted for teachers. Training for teachers may be too little, and too narrowly focused on using the computer rather than using it for teaching and learning across the curriculum.
Computer Communication		
Enables teachers to participate in larger professional communities, beyond their local ones. Provides access to databases, either on a local area network provided by the education authorities, or the Internet. Enables teachers to follow professional development programmes provided by remote institutions.	Can provide a wide range of multi-media materials, if the infrastructure (and bandwidth) permit. Supports a range of interaction, from formal to informal of varying group size. Can archive discussions for later use by other teacher.	Problems of access and cost in some countries. Requires an adequate infrastructure (electricity, telecommunications), affordable prices, supportive policy framework and investment of resources.

(Contd.)

Function in Teacher Education and Development	*Strengths*	*Limitations and Requirements*
	Allows teachers to participate widely and to exchange experience and materials in peer groups. Provides access to more sources of information and assistance, on topics from the specific ("How do I teach the new curriculum on environmental studies to Grade 3 children"?) to more general educational topics.	Requires a change in perceptions and practices in teaching and learning (in contrast to common perception that having computer communications will of itself improving the quality of teaching and learning). If lengthy print materials are produced through downloading, this may increase costs per copy over those of centralised print production and shift costs to the teacher, school or district. Requires training for effective use (often neglected). Requires considerable technical support.

APPENDIX VII

Teacher Education Institutions Recognised by NCTE

Madhya Pradesh Bhoj (Open) University

Name of Institution:	Madhya Pradesh Bhoj (Open) University
Address:	Bhopal (Open Uni.), Madhya Pradesh
Management:	Unaided
Affiliated to:	Madhya Pradesh Bhoj University
Medium of Instruction:	N.A.
Open to:	Co-education
Course: B.Ed. (DE)	
Course Status :	Recognised
Course Duration:	2 year
Current Intake:	500
Course Session	N.A.
Annual Tuition Fee:	N.A.
Minimum Eligibility for Admission:	N.A.
Selection for admission:	N.A.

For more information, please contact:

Regional Director,
Western Regional Committee (NCTE),
Manas Bhawan, Shyamla Hills,
Bhopal-462002,
Ph.No. : 0755-2530912(RD), 2739672(0)
Fax No.: 0755-2530912
Email: nctebhpl@born6.vsn.net.in

Jamia Millia Islamia (Centre For Dist and Open Lea.)

Name of Institution:	Jamia Millia Islamia (Centre For Dist and Open Lea.)
Address:	Jamia Nagar, New Delhi-110025, Delhi
Management:	University Department
Affiliated to:	Jamia Millia Islamia
Medium of Instruction:	N.A.
Open to:	Co-education
Course: B.Ed.(DE)	
Course Status :	Recognised Year of Recognition : 2003
Course Duration:	2 year
Current Intake:	500
Course Session	N.A.
Annual Tuition Fee:	N.A.
Minimum Eligibility for Admission:	N.A.
Selection for admission:	N.A.

For more information, please contact:

Regional Director,
Northern Regional Committee (NCTE),
A-46, Shanti Path,
Tilak Nagar,
Jaipur-302004,
Ph. No. : 0141-2620116(RD), 2623501(0)
Fax No.: 0141-2620116
Email: ncte@raj.nic.in

Tripura University, Directorate of Distance Education

Name of Institution:	Directorate of Distance Education
Address:	Tripura University, West Tripura Agartala-799004, Tripura Telephone:(0381)-22-2043(R), 22-5407(0)
Total No. of Teachers:	Full Time: 4, Part Time: 10
Year of Establishment:	1988
Management:	University Department
Affiliated to:	Tripura University, Agartala
Medium of Instruction:	ENGLISH
Open to:	Co-education
Course: B.Ed. (DE)	
Course Status :	Recognised
Course Duration:	2 year
Current Intake:	200
Course Session	July-June
Annual Tuition Fee:	Rs. 600
Minimum Eligibility for Admission:	Graduate In-service Teachers
Selection for admission:	Institutional

For more information, please contact:

Regional Director,
Eastern Regional Committee (NCTE),
E-15, Neel Kanth Nagar,
Nayapalli,
Bhubaneshwar-751 012
Ph. No. : 0674-2416156(RD), 2415793(0)
Fax No.: 0674-2414873
Email: ncteerc@hotmail.com

U.P. Rajarshi Tandon Open University

Name of Institution:	U.P. Rajarshi Tandon Open University
Address:	17, Maharshi Dayanand Marg, Thornhill Road, Allahabad-211001, Uttar Pradesh
Management:	Unaided
Affiliated to:	Rajarshi Tandon Open University
Medium of Instruction:	N.A.
Open to:	Co-education
Course: B.Ed. (DE)	
Course Status :	Recognised Year of Recognition : 2002
Course Duration:	2 year
Current Intake:	500
Course Session	N.A.
Annual Tuition Fee:	N.A.
Minimum Eligibility for Admission:	N.A.
Selection for admission:	N.A.

For more information, please contact:

Regional Director,
Northern Regional Committee (NCTE),
A-46, Shanti Path,
Tilak Nagar,
Jaipur-302004,
Ph. No. : 0141-2620116(RD), 2623601 (O)
Fax No.: 0141-2620116
Email: ncte@raj.nic.in

State-wise Distribution of DIETs, CTEs and IASEs on 31.03.2008

Sl. No.	*State/UT*	*No. of Distts*	*No. of DIETs/CTEs/ IASEs Sanctioned*			*No. of DIETs/CTEs/ IASEs Functional*		
			DIETs/ DRCs	*CTEs*	*IASEs*	*DIETs/ DRCs*	*CTEs*	*IASEs*
1.	Andhra Pradesh	23	23	8	2	23	8	2
2.	Arunachal Pradesh	15	11	0	o	6	0	0
3.	Assam	23	23	8	2	18	8	2
4.	Bihar	37	24	4	0	24	4	0
5.	Chhattisgarh	16	16	1	1	12	1	1
6.	Goa	2	1	0	0	1	0	0
7.	Gyiarat	25	26	8	2	26	8	2
8.	Haryana	19	19	0	1	19	0	1
9.	Himachal Pradesh	12	12	1	0	12	1	0
10.	Jammu & Kashmir	14	14	2	0	14	2	0
11.	Jharkhand	22	22	1	0	19	1	0
12.	Karnataka	27	22	1	0	19	1	0
13.	Kerala	27	27	9	2	27	9	2
14.	Madhya Pradesh	14	14	3	1	14	3	1
15.	Maharashtra	35	34	12	2	29	12	2
16.	Manipur	9	9		0	9	1	o
17.	Meghalaya	7	7	2	0	7	2	o
18.	Mizoram	8	8	0	1	8	0	1
19.	Nagaland	8	8	1	0	6	1	0
20.	Orissa	30	30	10	2	30	10	2
21.	Punjab	17	17	2	1	12	2	1
22.	Rajasthan	32	32	9	2	30	9	2
23.	Sikkim	4	3	0	0	1	0	0
24.	Tamil Nadu	30	29	5	2	29	5	2
25.	Tripura	4	4	1	0	4	1	0
26.	Uttar Pradesh	70	70	3	3	70	3	3
27.	Uttrakhand	13	13	3	1	13	3	1
28.	West Bengal	18	18	4	2	16	4	2
29.	A & N Islands	2	1	0	0	1	0	0
30.	Delhi	9	9	0	2	9	0	2
31.	Pondicherry	4	1	0	0	1	0	0
32.	Lakshadweep	1	1	0	0	1		0
33.	Daman & Diu	2	0	0	0	0	0	0
34.	Dadra & Nagar Havel	1	0	0	0	0	0	0
35.	Chandigarh	1	0	0	0	0	0	0
	Total	599	571	104	31	529	104	31

Bibliography

Anand, S. (1979), " *University without Walls*", Vikas Publishing, New Delhi.

Anandakrishnan, M. (2001), "Convergence of Knowledge System: Imperatives of Continuous Learning", *University News*, Vol. 39, No. 32, August.

Arger, G. and White, M. (1993), "An Approach to the Evaluation of Teaching and Learning in Japanese Distance Education", *Media and Technology for HRD*, Vol. 6, No. 1.

Arizona Learning Systems (1998), *"Preliminary Cost Methodology for Distance Learning"*. Arizona Learning Systems and the State Board of Directors for Community Colleges of Arizona.

Arora, G.L. and Pranati Panda (1999), "Restructuring Teacher Education—Need for Paradigm Shift", *University News*, Vol. 37, No. 20, May 17.

Avalos, B. (1991), *"Approaches to Teacher Education: Initial Teacher Training"*, London, Commonwealth Secretariat.

Beeby, C.E. (1966), *"The Quality of Education in Developing Countries"*, Cambridge Mass: Harvard University Press.

Biswal, B.N. (1979), *"A Study of Correspondence Education in Indian University"*, Ph.D. Thesis, CASE, Baroda.

Buch, M.B. (1997), *"5th Survey of Educational Research (1988-92)"*, Vol. I, NCERT, New Delhi.

Chale, E.M. (1993), *"Tanzania's Distance-teaching Programme"*, In Perraton H., (ed.), "Distance Education for Teacher Training", Routledge, London.

Chauhan, C.P.S. (2001), "Revitalizing Teacher Education", *University News*, Vol. 39, No. 32, August 6-12.

Chauhan, Poonam (2001), "Restructuring of Teacher Education for Quality Improvement", *University News*, Vol. 39, No. 53, December 31.

Chivore, B.R.S. (1993), *"The Zimbabwe Integrated Teacher Education Course"*, in Perraton H. 1993, (*Ibid*).

Clark, R.E. (1983), "Reconsidering Research on Learning from Media", *Review of Educational Research*, Vol. 53, No. 4, pp. 445-59.

Creed, Chalotte (2001), *"The Use of Distance Education for Teachers"*, Report for DFID, International Research Foundation for Open Learning, London.

Das, B.C. (1999), "A Model Approach to Teacher Training Programme: An Experiment", *University News*, Vol. 37, No. 22, May 31.

Dash, Nirod K. and Menon S.B. (2000) (eds.), *"Training of Professionals through Distance Education in South Asia."* Proceeding of the SAFDED International Workshop 1997 (Sponsored by IGNOU and UNESCO).

Datt, R. (1985), "Distance Education in India," *Journal of Higher Education*, Vol. 11, No. 2.

Department for International Development (2001),*"Imfundo: Partnership for IT in Education,"* Inception Report, London.

Goel, D.R. (2001), "Influences of Contemporary Society on Teacher Education", *University News*, Vol. 39, No. 50, December 10-16.

Greenland, J. (1983) (ed.), *"The in-service Training of Primary School Teacher in English-speaking Africa: A Report"*, Basingstoke ; Macmillan.

Gupta, M.L. (1978), *"Place of Correspondence Education in India's Economy,"* M.Phil. Thesis, University of Delhi.

Haque, Hasibul, *"Potential Role of Electronic Communication and Regional Network in South Asia for English Language Teacher Education Through Distance Mode"*.

Harichandan, D. (2000), *"Teacher Education in Maharashtra"*, In Teacher Education in India, Selection from *University News*, Association of Indian Universities, New Delhi.

Hulsmann, T. (2000), *"The Cost of Open Learning: A Handbook"*, Oldenburg; BIS, University of Oldenburg.

Joshi, Vibha and *et al.*, *"In-Service Training of Primary School Teachers through Distance Mode: IGNOU Experience"*.

Kabir, Shamsul, *"Teacher Education in Bangladesh through Distance Mode and Possibilities for Collaboration between Bangladesh Open University, Indira Gandhi National Open University and Allama Iqbal Open University".*

Khan, I. (1989), *"Teaching at a Distance,"* Delhi, Amar Prakashan.

Koul, B.N. (1988), *"Tutor comments, A Distance Teaching Technique"*, "In Studeis in Distance Education," Koul, B.N., Singh, B., Ansari, M.M. (ed.) Association of Indian Universities, New Delhi, pp. 39-52.

Khan, Riaz Shakir (1998), *"NCTE Initiatives for Quality Teacher Education"*, NCTE, New Delhi.

Lee, June (2001), *"Instructional Support for Distance Education and Faculty Motivation, Commitment, Satisfaction," BJET*, Vol. 32, No. 2.

Moon, B. and Leach, J. (1997), *"Towards a New Generation of Open Learning Programmes in Teacher Education: The Open University (UK) Pre-service Teacher Education Programme,"* paper presented to the Distance Education for teacher development colloquium, Global Knowledge 1997 Conference, Toronto, 22-25 June.

Mouli, Cherla Raja, *"Training University and College Teachers in India: An Eclectic Model".*

NCTE (1998), *"Policy Perspectives in Teacher Education: Critique and Documentation,"* Recommendations of various Commissions and Committees on Teacher Education, New Delhi.

Nielsen, H.D. and Tatto, M.T. (1993), *"Teacher Upgrading in Sri Lanka and Indonesia"* In Perraton (*Ibid*).

Pal, Suraksha (1999), "Excellence in Teacher Education: A Challenge," *University News*, Vol. 37, No. 27, July.

Panigrahi, S.C. and *et. al.* (2004), "Influences of Contemporary Society on Teacher Education," *University News*, Vol. 39, No. 50, December.

Passi, B.K. (2000), *"Innovative Teacher Education: A Pipe Dream,"* In Teacher Education in India, Selection from *University News*. Association of Indian Universities, New Delhi.

Perraton, H. (ed), (1993), *"Distance Education for Teacher Training"*, Routledge, London.

Perraton, H. (2000), *"Open and Distance Learning in the Developing World"*, Routledge, London.

Perraton, H. (2001), *"Quality and Standard of INSET Teacher Training by Open and Distance Learning,"* Paper presented to the Pan-African Dialouge on in-service teacher training by open and distance learning, Windhoek, Namibia, 9-12 July.

Perraton, H. and Creed, C. (1999), *"Distance Education Practice: Training and Rewarding Authors"*, London: DFID Education Research Series, No. 33.

Perraton, H. and Creed, C. (2000), *"Applying New Technologies and Cost-effective Delivery System in Basic Education"*, Thematic study for Education for all, Paris: UNESCO.

Quality Assurance Agency for Higher Education (1999), *"Distance Learning Guidelines,"* Gloucester (http://www.qaa.ac.uk/public/dlg/contents.htm, accessed 3 December 2001).

Ram Reddy, G. (1988), *"Distance Education—What, Why and How?"*, Studies in Distance Education; "Koul, B.N., Singh, B., Ansari, M.M. (ed) Association of Indian Universities, New Delhi, pp. 11-26.

Rathore, H.C.S., *"Preservice Training of Teachers through Distance Education: Critical Appraisal and Suggestions"*.

Robinson, Bernadotte and *et al.* (2003), *"Teacher Education through Open and Distance Learning"*, Routledge Falmer, New York.

Robinson, B. (1997), *"Distance Education for Primary Teacher Training in Developing Countries"* in Lynch, J. *et al.* (ed.) Innovations in Delivering Primary Education, Vol. III of Education and Development; Tradition and Innovation, London: Cassell.

Russell, T. and McPherson, S. (2001), *"Indicators of Success in Teacher Education: A Review and Analysis of Recent Research,"* Paper presented to Pan-Canadian Education Research Agenda Symposium on Teacher Education/Educator Training, Quebec: University Laval, 22-23 May.

Saha, Sujata (1997), "Quality Improvement of Teacher Education—A Future Perspective", *University News*, Vol. 37, No. 37, Sept. 13.

Sahoo, P.K., *"Professional Education for Teachers through Distance Education"*.

Shetty, Anitha D., "Networking in Teacher Education," *University News*, Vol. 37, No. 1, January 4.

Singh, R.P., Rana, G. (1999), "An Inquiry into the B.Ed. Programmes of the Indian Universities", *University News*, Vol. 37, No. 25, June 21.

Torres, R.M. (1996), *"Without the Reform of Teacher Education there will be no Reform of Education,"* Prospects, 26, 3:447-67.

UNESCO (2001), *"Teacher Education through Distance Learning: Technology, Curriculum, Cost, Evaluation,"* Summary of Case Studies, Education Sector, Higher Education Division, Teacher Education Section, Paris.

UNESCO (2002), *"Teacher Education Guidelines: Using Open and Distance Learning,"* Higher Education Division, Teacher Education Section, Paris.

Websites

UNESCO's education website contains a variety of downloadable material relevant to teacher education and the use of distance education: http://www.unesco.org/education/portal/e_learning/index.shtml.

On the E9 initiative, addressing the needs of the nine high-population countries at http://www.unesco.org/education/e9/publications

There is a training package to assist primary school teacher to improve their multi-grade teaching skills at: http://www.unesco.org/education /primary/teacher.shtml

The International Bureau of Education, also has a databank of innovative educational programmes including teacher education and distance education projects. The website is: www.ibe.unesco.org/international/datablanks/innodata/inno.htm

There is a website devoted to the needs of teacher run by UNICEF, containing articles opinions and researches likely to be of interest to teacher at: http://www.unicef.org/teacher/build.htm

The World Bank has set-up a Global Distance Education Net which contains paper on teaching and learning, technology, management, policy and programmes. The website is at: http://www1.worldbank.org/_vti_bin/shtml.dll/DistEd/index.html/map2

The World Bank has also set-up a Global Development Learning Network, an activity based at its training arm the World Bank Institute. Its activities are described at: http://www.gdln.org/

Information on its own research programmes in open and distance learning is available from the International Research Foundation For Open Learning at: http://www.col.org/irfol

The multi-site teacher education research project (MUSTER) run by the Center of International Education, University of Sussex has a website with downloadable research paper on teacher education in a group of which embraced the use of distance education in Malawi:http://www.sussex.ac.uk/usie/muster

A free bimontly newsletter on the use of information and communication technologies in education is produced by an American agency, Knowledge Enterprise Inc. The November/December 2000 issue focuses on the use of technology for teacher education. It is distributed electronically and is available at: http://www.TechKnowLogia.org

The British Department for International Development has set-up a project concerned with the deployment of information technologies to support education in Africa. Its website has a resource bank of information which is at: http://www.imfundo.org

A major source of information about open and distance learning is the International Centre for Distance Learning, housed at the British Open University. It has a conventional library and a website which gives acces to information about literature, courses, and institutions. The address is: http://icdl.open.ac.uk

Index